The Manchester A
book, is proud to hel
effort. The singular a
of decline in the conc

the original name for the collection of businesses and buildings on what is today's Main Street. These activities merit the recognition given them in this book.

A long-standing interest in Manchester's local history was expressed for many years by an historical interest group of the Manchester Township Library and its Historical Room. In 1976, as part of Manchester's flurry of Bicentennial activity, the group incorporated as the Manchester Area Historical Society. In 1982, the John Schneider Blacksmith Shop was purchased, at a nominal price, from Don Limpert who had saved it, along with much of Exchange Place, from further neglect and decay. Don also donated to the Historical Society many of the hand and machine tools which remained in the shop after its more than 100 years as a wagon factory and blacksmith shop.

Two main objectives of the Historical Society are to: (1) maintain and demonstrate the art of blacksmithing and (2) collect Manchester artifacts for museum display. The two objectives do not co-exist well in the same facility and site limitations preclude separating them in this historic building. It is hoped that proceeds from the book sales, which are generously being gifted to the Historical Society, can hasten the day that Don's long-standing dream of a history museum in the community of Manchester can be realized.

Don Limpert is a life member, and a past president, of the Manchester Area Historical Society.

Manchester Area Historical Society, established 1976

Manchester Area Historical Society
324 East Main Street
P. O. Box 56 Manchester MI 48158
mahs-info@manchesterareahistoricalsociety.org.

IF...

Also by Harry Macomber

*How the Bee Got Inside My Bib Overalls
and other farm stories from the 1940s and 1950s*

IF...
The oft-times colorful life and accomplishments of Manchester, Michigan's infamous black sheep–
DON LIMPERT

By Harry Macomber and Marsha Chartrand

River Pointe Publications • Milan, Michigan, USA

Copyright © 2009 Harry Macomber
& Marsha Johnson Chartrand
with Thomas Dodd

Published in the USA by
River Pointe Publications
P.O. Box 234
Milan, Michigan 48160
riverptpub@sbcglobal.net

All rights reserved

No part of this book may be reproduced or utilized
in any form or by any means, electronic or mechanical,
except in the context of reviews, without
prior written permission from the authors.

**Sales of this book to benefit the
Manchester Area Historical Society
324 East Main Street
P. O. Box 56 Manchester MI 48158**

DEDICATED

to those colorful individuals
we've been fortunate to meet on life's journey.
We are drawn to unusual characters, misfits and renegades–
those out-of-step, non-conformists who make life
so much more interesting. May they always persevere
and ever increase in number.
Society is all the richer for their having been born.

-Harry Macomber & Marsha Chartrand

ACKNOWLEDGEMENTS

Tom Dodd, editor

Jerry Holthouse, cover design

Special thanks to Hazel Proctor
for permitting the use of photos and captions
from her "Old Manchester Village"
prepared for the Village of Manchester
by Ann Arbor Federal Savings in 1974

IF...

The oft-times colorful life and accomplishments of Manchester, Michigan's infamous black sheep– DON LIMPERT
by Harry Macomber & Marsha Chartrand

"IF..." by Rudyard Kipling....................1
Introduction..3
Prologue... 6
A Pair of Incorrigibles........................ 15
A Lone Voice for Preservation...........18
"Progress"...21
The Perils of Business........................ 23
The Early Years..................................25
Spiegel Years..................................... 29
Purchasing Buildings......................... 31
Changes on Main Street.....................37
The Black Sheep................................ 46
Mill Pond Apartments 53
Manchester Mill................................. 55
Other Venues......................................60
Hardcore and Untrainable..................63
The Bidwell Exchange.......................66
Blacksmith Shop................................ 68
Clinton Hotel......................................72
The Enterprise....................................76
Center of the Universe........................81
A Commitment to History..................85
Nominations.......................................87
Civil War Collection..........................95
Rudy Lorin...98
Open House..99
Genealogy...100
Epilogue..108
Afterwords..110

Macomber & Chartrand

IF *by Rudyard Kipling   (Don Limpert's favorite poem)*

If you can keep your head when all about you
Are losing theirs and blaming it on you;
If you can trust yourself when all men doubt you,
But make allowance for their doubting too;
If you can wait and not be tired by waiting,
Or, being lied about, don't deal in lies,
Or, being hated, don't give way to hating,
And yet don't look too good, nor talk too wise;

Kipling

If you can dream - and not make dreams your master;
If you can think - and not make thoughts your aim;
If you can meet with triumph and disaster
And treat those two imposters just the same;
If you can bear to hear the truth you've spoken
Twisted by knaves to make a trap for fools,
Or watch the things you gave your life to broken,
And stoop and build 'em up with wornout tools;

If you can make one heap of all your winnings
And risk it on one turn of pitch-and-toss,
And lose, and start again at your beginnings
And never breathe a word about your loss;
If you can force your heart and nerve and sinew
To serve your turn long after they are gone,
And so hold on when there is nothing in you
Except the Will which says to them: "Hold on";

If you can talk with crowds and keep your virtue,
Or walk with kings - nor lose the common touch;
If neither foes nor loving friends can hurt you;
If all men count with you, but none too much;
If you can fill the unforgiving minute
With sixty seconds' worth of distance run
Yours is the Earth and everything that's in it,
And - which is more - you'll be a Man my son!

If...

Macomber & Chartrand

*"If you can keep your head when all about you
Are losing theirs and blaming it on you…"*

INTRODUCTION

Families don't build monuments to honor their black sheep. Neither do communities. Regardless of how talented, or how far-reaching their accomplishments, the renegades of society rarely get their just due in terms of public recognition.

The fact is, most humans find comfort in conformity. Peer pressure and popular acceptance are the guidelines that make life's journey one of smooth sailing and comfort. Only rarely does an individual arrive who not only lives, but who seems to thrive by dancing outside that comfort zone. The Black Sheep. One such man is Don Limpert.

Don Limpert arrived in Manchester, Michigan just as an era of small town merchants providing the necessities of life was coming to an end. Shopping malls and mega stores were just in their beginning stages. Manchester merchants like Waldo Marx Dry Goods, Walt Schaible Men's Wear, Herb Widmayer Hardware & Furniture, Haller Meats, Lannom's Five & Dime, and L.V. Kirk Appliance & Electrical Service were slipping into obsolescence. These elderly men, who had become pillars of their community in the years following the Great Depression, were the last of their kind. No sons or daughters or any other young men and women were waiting in the wings to step into those small-town merchants' shoes. Retirement went hand in hand with going-out-of-business signs in the windows.

The once ornate, now deteriorating Main Street buildings were slowly being vacated. Many could be purchased for a fraction of their prior value. While many saw these buildings as a growing liability, Don Limpert saw them as unlimited opportunities. Not only did Limpert see the opportunity, he saw their threatened destruction as a great tragedy.

His very first confrontation with local officials was over the demolition of the Dresselhouse & Davidter building, a harness shop, hardware and Case dealership, building next door to the bank. Limpert lost that first battle and a giant cavity in Manchester's character appeared overnight. In fact, it is the banking industry itself that was one of the biggest forces in the rape and destruction of small town architecture and character, a fact sadly in evidence when viewing what is now the Comerica bank building today with its modern first floor and turn-of-the-century floors remaining above. Limpert likens it to "a 90-year-old woman with a face lift."

Don Limpert began to buy buildings in Manchester in 1963. Using his own unique style, he re-did them combining old and new into a seamless style of historic beauty and modern function. He not only created new uses for the main floor spaces, but utilized the upper floors as living quarters. He also did something even the original owners of those buildings hadn't. He made the backs that faced the alley as attractive as the fronts.

When I arrived on the scene in 1965, Limpert had already provoked the ire of many town officials. I heard the stories long before I actually met the man behind them. Most centered on his ignoring the red tags that seemed to appear overnight on his buildings. Since no one had invested time and money into any Main Street buildings in years, the building codes and inspectors were caught off guard. Here was an outsider who not only didn't ask permission but made improvements with amazing speed. To make matters worse, Limpert, a building contractor himself, knew more about codes than most of the inspectors. He ignored the efforts to rein him in.

In truth, Don Limpert almost single-handedly reshaped Manchester's future. He showed how to revitalize a dying town long before it became an anthem for small towns facing similar fates across America

The stories I was hearing only fueled my interest in meeting this trouble-maker. One Sunday afternoon I drove out to his farm to introduce myself. That was the start of a long, colorful, engaging, and enjoyable friendship.

Now, all these years later, it is time to tell Don Limpert's story. If any man deserves to be so recognized, it is Don Limpert.

- Harry Macomber

If…

PROLOGUE
A photo essay of scenes of the Manchester, Michigan townscape through the years

Hazel Proctor has kindly given permission for the use of photographs of nearly 150 years of downtown life from her 1974 publication "Old Manchester Village" published by Ann Arbor Federal Savings for the Village of Manchester.

1868

The village center was thriving. The walkway across the bridge has solid wooden sides to protect pedestrians from the splashing mud from horses and wagons.

1872
Birds-eye view of Manchester Washtenaw County, Mich.

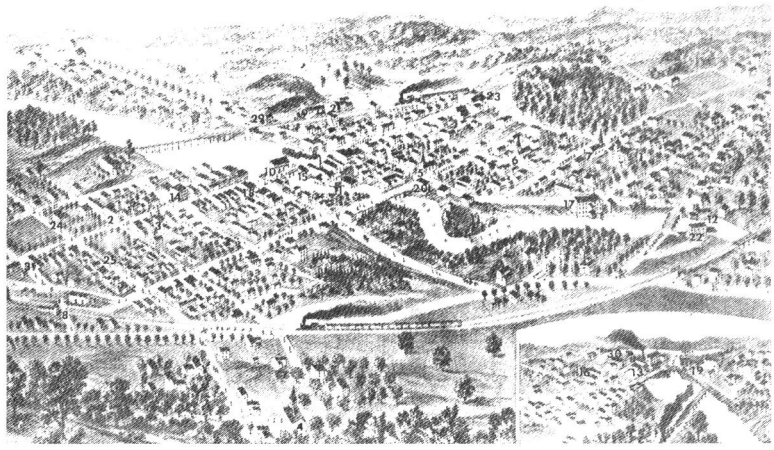

This picture was given to the Manchester Township Library by Arthur Jenter. It is an enlarged photograph of a sketch originally owned by Miss Julia Kirchhofer. (Mrs. Frank S. Spafard has kindly made up this log of information.)

Circa 1873

Exchange Place

If...
Circa 1880

The Haeussler-Kingsley Drug Store also sold books, stationery, school supplies, lamps, some hardware, and groceries. Note the boardwalk, and cobblestone street.

Macomber & Chartrand
Circa 1885

J. Fred Schaible Dry Goods & Grocery Store. Fred is on the right.
Note the kerosene street lamp.

1887

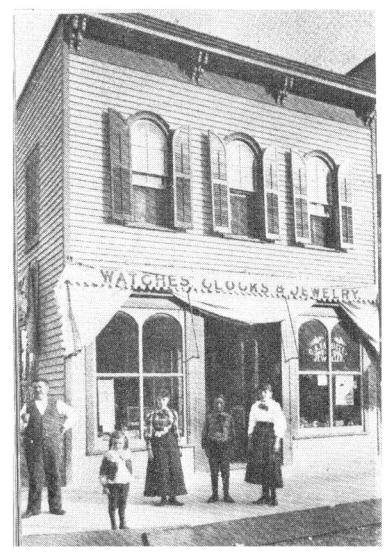

G. A. Fausel Jewelry Store—corner of
Riverside and Exchange Place.
The family lived above the store.

If...
1890

View from Water Tower Hill—House in left foreground is Towne's Apple Drying House. During the fall apple season the women of the village would peel apples in the factory. Towne dried apples were renowned througout the county. At center of photo is the ice house with its chute, which was used to pull the cut ice from the river.

Circa 1892

Electric street lights brighten Exchange Place. J.H. Kingsley, operator of the Premium Mills on the River Raisin, charged the village $700 a year for fifty 32-candle lights. The bulbs were replaced by lowering the lamp by the rope and pulley seen at the top of the picture.

1894

Union Bank block. Masonic Hall is on the third story.

Circa 1900

By the turn of the century, an iron bridge covered the River Raisin.

If...
1906

Looking east on the north side. The three-story hotel in the foreground boasted running water, which was drawn to a tank on the third floor by a windmill. The public baths in the hotel were a popular weekend occupation of the villagers.

1906

Wagons parked on the north side looking west on Exchange Place. The canvas on the grocery delivery wagon in the center advertised the "specials."

1908

Villagers view the damage of the broken dam from the Main Street bridge

1925

Exchange Place was the address of only the main business district, while Jefferson Street was the eastern continuation of the main road through the village and Jackson Street was the western section.

If...

1925

Exchange Place's name changed to Main Street

North on River Raisin toward Mill and Dam

Don with Young Dudley

Mature Dudley casts a long shadow over the affairs of the Limpert Empire

A PAIR OF INCORRIGIBLES

Don and Ms. Dudley DoRight

As I sat contemplating where to start with Don Limpert's story, I was reflecting not only on his many accomplishments, but on the things that make him a unique personality. A black and white listing of his achievements would look only slightly different than many other individual entrepreneurs we could name.

These stories will intentionally try to reflect Don's unique, personal way of doing things. As his friend for some 45-odd years, I have developed some insight on just what makes him tick. I plan on sharing that in the following stories.

The entire time I've known him, Don has had animals. Even growing up in the city of Royal Oak, his family had a milk cow. He also had grandparents who were farmers and Don spent many summers helping on their farm. Anyone who has ever visited Don on one of the farms he has owned in the area, invariably had to wipe "fowl poop" off their shoes upon leaving. His menagerie of free-range assorted fowl was

If...

almost as much a trademark as his hat or broom.

This first story is about a dog. Fate must have guided an impulse purchase at the Hillsdale Auction. Thinking he had gotten a free male puppy, Don learned differently upon arriving home. Not only was she female, but she also had his un-trainable personality.

Ms. Dudley

One thing you quickly learn when first meeting Don Limpert is that it is hard to hold your own in a conversation with him; he can dominate almost any exchange. His grasp of issues and his ability to articulate his views make him a formidable verbal force whether it is with a few friends or at a crowded public meeting.

He does, however, occasionally meet his match. One such match was a dog named Ms. Dudley DoRight.

I first met Ms. Dudley when I met Don at the coffee shop in Manchester one morning in the early 1990s. As I parked and walked past Don's truck with its trademark broom, I saw a dog inside. As I walked past, it rose and growled. When I glanced inside, I was stunned by the sight. The seat back and cushion were in shambles. It looked like it had been attacked by a pride of mountain lions.

When I asked Don what had happened, he just grinned. Ms. Dudley, it seems, was an Alpha female in the truest sense of the word. Any dog she spied walking past or in another nearby vehicle brought out her territorial instincts. Unable to confront and state her dominance from behind the glass windows, she displayed her passion for leadership by attacking the only thing available: the cushions, arm rests, door panels, etc.

It wasn't long before Don's seat behind the steering wheel

consisted of bare springs and a piece of old carpet to cover them. "She only tore up my seat, not her own," he says. "I tried to repair the seat with bungee cords. She'd grab them and tear them off."

Dudley also managed to occasionally shrink the number of fowl who shared her space on the farm.

Don just smiled at my shock over the condition of his truck interior. I—or anyone else—would have left that dog home. Not Don. These two were on equal footing and neither would back down. This was clearly a situation of mutual respect and admiration of parallel personalities.

Don had the upholstery redone twice with the same result. Ms. Dudley finally passed away in December of 2006, after 15 years with Don.

Don still gets a twinkle in his eyes when he talks about his many years with the un-trainable Ms. Dudley. "She was very loyal to me," he says.

A new dog now shares his companionship. Kaiser is more mellow than Ms. Dudley was. Come to think of it, Don has mellowed a little too.

If...

*Downtown Manchester in the 1950s:
Main Street was beginning to look a bit grim*

*"If you can trust yourself when all men doubt you,
but make allowance for their doubting too"*

A LONE VOICE FOR PRESERVATION

America's history for the most part has always been that of a nation thriving on change, innovation, and creating something new. Since we have such a short history compared to the mostly European countries we came from, there has been little regard for preservation.

That was true when Don first arrived in Manchester in 1963. Urban renewal was under way. Old buildings were being torn down to make way for a new way of acquiring everyday goods and services. Small family-owned specialty stores were fading out and new shopping centers were replacing them.

While Manchester for the most part may have lagged behind in this transition, the local bank was looking ahead. Union Savings Bank was not alone in wanting to modernize. They wanted to be forward-looking as the automobile age hit full stride. Banks all over the country were assessing their cramped locations in the hearts of small towns. Many acquired the increasingly deserted Main Street buildings adjoining them. The goal was to make way for additional parking and the newest innovation: drive-through banking.

Shortly after acquiring his first building, Don learned the bank was planning to tear down the store just one door away from his building. He spoke out against it. No one listened. He later learned that this former hardware store was just the first the bank hoped to acquire with an eye toward future expansion. Most of that side of East Main Street was vulnerable.

Anyone traveling through small towns even today can see the evidence of what happened during this government-sponsored and financed Urban Renewal program. Many ornate, beautiful old buildings fell victim to the wrecking ball. Huge gaps appeared in small downtowns all over America, resulting in a tragic loss of character.

Banks wield tremendous power in small communities. Very few political or even average citizens are going to oppose any plan for bank expansion. Those who do may face economic reprisal if they ever need future financial backing.

The chairman of the Board at Union Savings Bank at the time was James Hendley. Soft-spoken, he still wielded enormous power in that position. He could dictate the outcome of issues with just a few phone calls. Don, the brash outsider, lost that first battle and the building was torn down. A power struggle ensued, out of public view, between Don and the bank president. However, Don managed to save the rest of those downtown buildings by purchasing them one by one.

Two things on Don's side were his talent for restoration and the respect he garnered from a man who owned several downtown buildings. That man was Dick Way. Had a friend of Jim Hendley owned those buildings instead, Manchester would

If...

look vastly different today.

While Don may have been at the forefront of restoring and saving historic buildings, other preservationists across the country were increasingly appalled at the loss of these beautiful and still functional old buildings. Common sense and the economic feasibility of restoration over destruction finally sank in.

Don, in his stubborn and outspoken way, was a pioneer in fighting Urban Renewal and showing small communities what was possible with these old downtown buildings. Even now, in 2009, he is still being sought out by other small towns in Michigan who seek his help in doing something similar to what he did in Manchester some forty years ago.

Mayors' Day, May 20, 1957. Local politicians sometimes resisted Limpert's ideas. Left to right: Bennet Root, R.B. Haeussler, Fred Lehman, Arthur Jenter, Ed Dresselhouse, Tosselo Knorp, George Merriman

"PROGRESS" COMES TO MANCHESTER

In the 1960s, "urban renewal" threatened to displace the original central business district of Manchester. Downtowns across America were turning into boarded-up "plywood cities" as off-center shopping malls began to grow in what were once cornfields. While some romanticized about a preservation ethic, others merely saw these nineteenth century commercial buildings as old-fashioned and embarrassing.

According to the principle of entropy, everything falls apart, and in that context it appeared Manchester was completely up to date.

If...

The Exchange Place Bridge over the River Raisin had seen the railroad come and go to serve the mill at the middle of the central business district.

Top-quality retail stores were closing up as the older generation retired. Waldo Marx was one local businessman who appreciated Limpert's efforts.

This livery stable, located behind the Standard Oil station on Clinton Street, did not make the transition into serving the transportation industry.

Long-time businesses faded away as clientele shifted their loyalty to suburban malls. The new generation went away to earn an MBA and started working for big corporations.

Plans were being made for knocking down 19th century commercial buildings to create larger parking lots, but not many shoppers were looking for parking places in the downtown district anyway.

Joe Weiss's Red Bird cobbler's shop didn't wait for either Urban Renewal or Don Limpert; it tumbled into the River Raisin and disappeared on its own

"Or, being lied about, don't deal in lies"

THE PERILS OF BUSINESS ON THE RIVERBANK

In the 1920s, Railroad Street (now Adrian Street) in Manchester was the site of several local tradesmen. Among them were The Southern Washtenaw Mill, Dr. Ackerson the veterinarian, John Roller's furniture store and undertaker, and Joe Weiss, a "cobbler," who did shoemaking and repair. Prior to the cobbler's business being located there, the building had housed a butcher shop. According to Nathaniel Schmid's 1921 poetic description of village businesses fifty years prior, "Going South on Railroad Street is the Red Bird, where Joe Weiss is at work. Nicholas Stringham there sold all kinds of fresh meat and also salt pork."

If...

Weiss, a bachelor who lived with his mother in a frame house on the southeast corner of Beaufort and Duncan Streets, was a sociable man, who enjoyed dancing and often squired ladies to dances at the Arbeiter hall. He was described as short and "broad, but not heavy," by the late Herb Widmayer, who owned the hardware downtown.

Widmayer recalled Joe bringing a turtle caught from the river, for a turtle soup dinner to share with Herb and his wife, Isabel. "He hung it out back of the hardware by the tail, on the outdoor toilet, and started cutting it up," Herb said. "I suppose it was good, but all I could taste was river bottom."

Joe's business on Railroad Street was housed in a two-story building with a basement, built on log supports or stilts on the steep river bank. The machinery Weiss used had a line shaft for grinding the leather to make well-crafted boots and shoes. The line shaft was powered by an electric motor which vibrated the old building at times.

People often stopped in to visit with Joe as he worked; Anton Vogt of the handle factory and Ora Logan were two frequent visitors.

One evening, Joe had evidently gone off for dinner at about 7 or 7:30 p.m. and as Mr. Leeman stood on the bridge at that moment, he saw the cobbler's building fall to the river bank. Moments later, there was only a cloud of dust hanging in the air from the plaster inside the building.

"He was out of business in a hurry," Widmayer recalled.

It was fortunate for Weiss and his many friends and visitors that the building was unoccupied at the time, as they would surely have been severely injured or killed. Joe Weiss never re-opened his cobbling business, but retired thereafter.

No news account of this calamity has been found in old issues of the *Manchester Enterprise*, so an exact date for this event cannot be determined.

The Weiss building was located on the edge of a 32' x 50' addition to the Mill, constructed about 1975 or -6. Don recalls seeing remnants of the foundation when working on Mill restoration in the early 1980s.

Limpert's company vehicles were never very flashy

*"Or, being hated, don't give way to hating,
And yet don't look too good, nor talk too wise"*

THE EARLY YEARS

Don was born Donald Edwin Limpert on May 7, 1927 at Groveport, Ohio in his grandparent's farmhouse. He was the eldest of five children. His father Frank was a dentist in the Detroit area; his mother Mary, a farm girl from Ohio. Royal Oak at that time was still a rural area and consequently the family had chickens and a milk cow. Being the oldest child, the duties of taking care of the animals fell to Don. Summers were spent partly on his grandparents' farm in Groveport. He remembers those days with great fondness. Threshing, haying and the old Rumley Oil Pull Tractor, all elicit memories of his days on the farm in the 1930s and early 1940s.

The Limpert family traces itself back to Germany. In fact, Don's father wrote a book of Limpert history including details

If...

as far back as the 1600 [*see page 100*]. Many papers and even a large wooden chest that early immigrants brought with them to America are in Don's possession for safe keeping, someday to be passed down to his sons. His great grandfather had settled in Section 2 of Freedom Township and family members are buried in the cemetery at Salem Lutheran Church in nearby Scio Township. Don's family is rich in recorded history going back five generations in Michigan's Washtenaw County. Don is the last one.

Early headquarters

Don graduated from high school in 1945 and he was confirmed in St. Paul's Lutheran Church in Royal Oak. During his high school years Don worked for his father doing cleaning and maintenance work at his office in Detroit.

After graduation he joined the J.A. Utley Construction Company as an apprentice carpenter. The company was then remodeling the Cranbrook School buildings in Bloomfield Township, north of Detroit. In 1947 Don and a friend decided to see a little of this country. He took a leave of absence and the two traveled to Texas City, Texas, where they worked in construction, then traveled to Houston, doing bridge work on a highway. Then it was on to El Paso, Texas. A little later they ended up in Reno, Nevada which Don notes, "did not have much of a downtown."

They finally ended up in Los Angeles, California. They got jobs helping build the new Los Angeles Times office building. Don remembers that streetcars were the way to get around. He paid $5 per week for a room and a big meal could be bought for 90 cents. While on that project, Don was teamed with a third-generation German man named Otto who did the trim work for the building. Otto, a bachelor, was a WWII veteran and was one of several master carpenters Don credits with teaching him much about the building trade.

First truck   *First fleet*

Don's friend left to get married. Don was twenty years old and a little homesick. He left Los Angeles on his twenty-first birthday, and drove back to Michigan to celebrate. The trip, with no stops, took four days.

Back home and still wanting his independence, Don bought a lot in Royal Oak for $250 and started his first house in 1948. His later reputation for re-using old stuff started there. He got many of his building materials by scrounging and salvaging. He finished the house in the fall of that year and lived in it alone. He chuckles recalling how it became sort of a "den of iniquity" with many young men bringing their girl friends there. Being unable to control things, Don sold the house.

Don was reading the paper one day and noticed an ad that said Argentina needed construction carpenters. It sounded interesting, so Don made plans to check it out. Those plans got interrupted one morning when he was taking a walk.

The walk was necessary because Don had stayed out late and partied too hard the night before. As he was out walking, he noticed a cute girl mowing the lawn. A smile led to conversation. She was divorced and the mother of two small children. She and her mother were both good cooks and, as dating got under way, the plans for Argentina were abandoned.

The young lady's name was Rita Sneller Parry. Planning for marriage and becoming an instant father, Don bought a vacant lot from his father and started construction on a second house. He and Rita tied the knot on August 19, 1950 and moved in. They couldn't afford furniture, so Don built the cabinets himself.

If...

Laying a foundation for the future. Limpert's work continued at the Rysinga Manufacturing Company, Detroit, 1953

During this time Don's day job was as superintendent for a construction company. He bought a second lot from his Dad and built his third house, into which the family moved.

After selling his second house, his family was growing and Don bought a 3-1/2 acre lot in Troy Township near Livernois and 16 Mile Road for $6500. He started his fourth house. A daughter, Renee, was born October 8, 1951 but lived only a short time. She was a blue baby and back then doctors could not save them. Son Ryan was born on November 5, 1952 and Scott on August 1, 1954.

The formula worked. Don and Rita's family had grown to six by 1960 with the additions of Ryan, Denise, William Bruce, and Scott.

*"If you can dream - and not make dreams your master:
If you can think - and not make thoughts your aim"*

THE SPIEGEL YEARS

Starting on his own, by May 1955, Don's "business sense" was firmly in place and he was ready to start his own company. His transition to being his own boss—responsible for the outcome from start to finish—went smoothly. His reputation for getting things done on time and on budget was already well established, so much so that he found businesses from whom he purchased supplies recommending him to potential customers.

A catalog store project in Ypsilanti

At first, he did mostly remodeling. It was a lumber company that recommended Don to the Spiegel catalog executives who were looking for a contractor to remodel existing downtown buildings into mail order facilities. He went on to work for the Spiegel Company from 1958 to 1968.

With retail in the flux of change, Spiegel started expanding rapidly across the country. This job took Don from Omaha, Nebraska to New York State. He would arrive in a new town and immediately hire a crew to redo the acquired building according to Spiegel specs.

Don recalls that he always found his new work crew by talking to suppliers and word-of-mouth as one sub-contractor would recommend another. The average time for Don to complete the renovation was one month.

As he began traveling to other states working for Spiegel, Don looked at properties each chance he got. While work-

If...

ing on a property in Hagerstown, Maryland, Don discovered an old run-down pre-Civil War mansion sitting on 212 acres. It was located in nearby Shepherdstown, West Virginia. It even had a cannonball still stuck in the brick wall. Don made an offer but backed out at the last minute. His young family didn't want to move that far away from everyone they knew in Royal Oak. "I still wish I'd brought that," says Don today. "I caved; the one and only time!"

Don smiles at the memory. He says that had he moved there he would probably have done work in Shepherdstown instead of Manchester. It is now a lovely renovated river town only an hour and a half from Washington, D.C.

He was involved with Spiegel for ten years, the last of which saw the closing of some of the stores he had renovated. Malls were rapidly expanding with convenience and free parking. Old downtowns were dying.

Don was also contracting work in the Detroit area. It was mostly contracts for small factory buildings and again it was his reputation that kept him busy. Luckily, Don did re-discover Manchester; his ancestors had farmed not far away.

He purchased his first building in Manchester from Dick Way for office space and his wife Rita opened an antique shop in the front. Antiques were a love they shared and with Don's skill at restoration from stripping the old finish off to repairing it quickly became part of their business.

It was in this busy world I first met Don. I remember visits in his office, blueprints spread out on tables where we'd talk politics, and future plans for Manchester. Little did I know that over time he would own and renovate many of the buildings on Main Street. A few he did for the owners, but most he purchased, remodeled and then re-sold.

From the Spiegel years, Don says that he learned a sense of how demographics dictate the future, as well as the fact that you can still get prime real estate in these old downtowns.

An interesting aside to settling in Manchester is that his eye for history and love of old buildings was in full bloom. Plus, as he notes, the Limperts are known as "wanderers."

*Downtown Manchester, Michigan: the stage where
much of Don Limpert's story is told*

*"If you can meet with triumph and disaster
And treat those two imposters just the same"*

Purchasing the buildings on Main Street

No master plan to almost single-handedly lead the restoration of Manchester's downtown was on Don Limpert's mind when he inquired about purchasing a single building for his office. He was told that Dick Way, a long-time Manchester businessman, had one for sale. It was vacant at the time and located at 115 E. Main. The year was 1963 and Don soon found himself the owner of his first Main Street building.

It served as office, antique shop, carpenter shop, furniture restoration facility, and storage for the growing number of "treasures" in the way of antiques he and Rita had been collecting. The family moved into the second floor where they lived—or "camped" as Don remembers—during construction

If...

Town Hall, circa 1876
The original town hall is now privately owned, having previously housed the Manchester Fire and Police Departments and both Village and Township offices.

of the house on their new farm on Mahrle Road.

Don said he had seen Troy Township get "raped" by urban growth and renewal and did not want to bring up his family in such an atmosphere. He saw the upper middle class kids getting into drugs, and didn't want that for his kids. Although Don had never seen Manchester, and didn't know a soul there, he saw a small ad in the *Detroit Free Press* offering 80 acres for $8,000 on Mahrle Road in Manchester Township. He met the realtor, and built one of the first new houses in the township in at least 50-60 years. He and his family moved out to their new house on Mahrle Road just before Thanksgiving in 1963.

The last homes built in the village, coincidentally, included Don's current house on Parr Street that was built in 1954 by

115 E. Main Street antique shop

the Thorntons, who had bought the old Ford building, and one on Washington St. that was built by "Mo" Schaible, a car dealer in town, also in the '50s.

His first purchase on Main Street, 115 E. Main, Don actually sought out the owner. Most of his later purchases were from owners of buildings seeking Don out to see if he'd be interested in theirs as well. A respect for Don's ability took root among the business and building owners. Even as controversy grew over Don's ignoring the village building department's red tags on his work, that respect for his ability remained true. As others began to realize the potential in those old buildings, the owners invariably sought out Don and offered them to him first. The one exception was when Don offered to buy the Widmayer Hardware store when Herb Widmayer retired. Herb had originally agreed to sell the hardware building to Don, but then sold to Sam Beal instead. Herb's sister-in-law, Hazel, who owned the furniture store across the street, was rumored to have told Herb that Don "owned enough" buildings already. It was in her will that her own building could never be sold to Don Limpert.

His next purchase was 111 E. Main, owned by Bob Hamilton. It was empty in 1966 when I rented the downstairs from Don to open a printing shop. Having never owned a business and a little unsure financially about starting one, Don offered encouragement in the form of a one-year lease with the first six months free.

Next came 109 E. Main, also purchased from Dick Way. Don now owned three buildings in a row. He re-did the second floors on all three building as apartments. To enhance the

If...

Antiques in the front

Office in the back

rear entrance to the apartments, Don built a deck across the back. By the time he finished, the back entrance was an attractive courtyard and he had no trouble renting those apartments as quickly as they were finished.

A major controversy arose as Don completed the apartments, however. He was paying three water/sewer bills, one for each building. Village Council had passed a new water ordinance which they interpreted as meaning they could charge a minimum bill for each separate apartment. Don took issue and refused to pay the extra charges. This went on for months with neither side giving in. It finally came to a head in 1968 when Don bought the Sportsman's Tavern building from Lawrence Bross. The deal included the liquor license. The transfer of that license, however, required a vote by Village Council. Those who felt Don had thumbed his nose at their rules long enough finally held the ace card: without the liquor license, all Don would be buying was another building.

I had been elected to Council in 1968 so I was part of this scenario. Being Don's friend, I worked at getting a compromise. The details are fuzzy after all these years but I do remember Don agreed to pay a token amount of the back water bills and Council agreed to amend the water ordinance. It had been Don's stand all along that it was not legal as written.

Don now owned four buildings in a row. The latest one housed an old farmers' tavern called the Sportsman's Tavern that he would eventually re-do into an upscale restaurant/bar called The Black Sheep Tavern.

On the opposite side of Main Street, Don's first purchase was a building that had housed Marx and Marx Women's

Limpert addresses Village Council

Village Council deliberates    *Manchester citizens look on*

Clothing for many years. In 1971 Waldo Marx approached Don about buying this building and Don quickly sealed the deal. A short time later, Dick Way again approached Don and offered to sell buildings 118, 120 and 130. These were the last buildings Way owned as he was retiring and had closed his bakery. Don recalls he walked through the buildings with Dick; the two men shook hands, and Don had three more buildings. He rented the old bakery space to Chuck King who ran the bakery for several years. In 2009 it still houses a bakery and coffee shop. Don's last purchase on that side of downtown's Main Street was the building at 104 E. Main owned by Simon Steele.

The man who had started out inquiring about a single building for his office now owned nine buildings in the heart of Manchester's downtown. Don's creative flair for making his buildings attractive was in full bloom. He added more apart-

If...

FIVE DOLLARS FINE FOR RIDING OR DRIVING ON THIS BRIDGE FASTER THAN A WALK BY ORDER OF HIGHWAY COM.

*This warning sing hung in the Village Hall for many years.
"By order of Highway Com." was probably not a "dot-com"*

ments and more importantly, he re-did the rears of these buildings too, making a vast improvement in the look and feel of the downtown. He demolished two old buildings behind 109, 111, 115 and 117 and installed a paved parking lot that was lit by real gaslights along one side.

On the north side, behind all of the buildings from the river to Adrian Street, the other owners—plus the Village—joined Don in improving the backs of the entire block. Each paid $1000 to clean and install paving and cement steps. The total amount raised was $14,000, which paid for all materials and paving. Don did the clearing for free. He remembers it as sort of a miracle that all of the business owners worked together to improve an entire block.

Downtown Manchester went through many changes

Anyone who has ever rehabilitated an historic building knows there's little time and energy left over to photograph "before" and "after" shots. These examples came from many sources, never thinking they would be assembled here.

128-130 EAST MAIN after

If...

109 EAST MAIN (1970S)

109 EAST MAIN (2000)

Macomber & Chartrand
110 EAST MAIN before

110 EAST MAIN after

If...
110 EAST MAIN today

118-120 EAST MAIN (1960s)

118-120 EAST MAIN
(1980s) (2000s)

If...
115-117 EAST MAIN

1968   **1971**

The rehabilitation of 117 East Main Street became, for many, the signature project of Don's efforts in Manchester. When he purchased the bar in November 1968, it was known as the Sportsman's Tavern. Don purchased the building and business from Lawrence Bross even while the local bank was eyeing it for expansion of their drive-through banking center and parking lot.

He ran the bar just as it was until the end of the year, and spent a month renovating it in his own style. In early 1969, the business re-opened as the Black Sheep Tavern.

In 1970, Don saw a need to expand into the first Main Street building he had purchased at 115 East Main. Originally, he had set up his antique shop at that site. He expanded the kitchen and created a dining room at 115, while the adjacent room at 117 encompassed the bar and a more informal eating area where people could wait to be seated.

From the beginning of the Black Sheep, Don employed a series of vaudeville-style piano players to entertain customers.

The Black Sheep was sold to Chris and Tim Hoover in 1976. See more on Don's Black Sheep years in the following chapter.

Macomber & Chartrand
130 EAST MAIN before

If...
130 EAST MAIN after

130 EAST MAIN today

Macomber & Chartrand
110 EAST MAIN

Even alley views were improved

Backside before 　　　　　　*Backside after*

If...

Black Sheep Tavern in its heyday, 1970s

*"If you can make one heap of all your winnings
And risk it on one turn of pitch-and-toss..."*

THE BLACK SHEEP

It may be a significant irony that the first building Don purchased in Manchester—115 E. Main Street—is still marked with the original 1970s sign that hung in front of the Black Sheep Tavern.

The Black Sheep, under Don's ownership, was a landmark in downtown Manchester and a drawing card for people from throughout Southeastern Michigan in the early 70s. Weeknights and weekends, Main Street's business district was filled from one end to the other with cars whose destination was The Black Sheep Tavern.

"When I bought my first building, I needed a location for

Before: Sportsman's Bar

Sportsman's Bar: the largest chain of non-franchised bars in the world

my business," Don says. "I had already bought the Mahrle Road property, and was working on building the house. I saw the empty building (at 115 E. Main) and it took me two weeks to find out who owned it—no one would tell me. I contacted a Realtor, Hugh Sutton, and he would say he'd get back to me.

"I had never met Dick Way before, but he saw me in front of that building one day and said, 'I hear you are looking for a building to buy. I own this one; would you like to look at it?"

Like most of Don's subsequent deals, this first one in Manchester was closed within hours over a conversation and a handshake. He used the building for a carpenter shop, and later turned it into an antique shop, which Rita ran. The family lived in an apartment he built upstairs, because he had found there were no apartments in Manchester at the time, only rooms in houses owned by elderly ladies.

In 1968, the Sportsman's Bar next door at 117 E. Main, which had been in existence since 1873, came up for sale. By this time, Don already owned several buildings on both sides of Main Street, and Lawrence Bross, the owner of

If...

115-117 EAST MAIN, Sloat Tavern, Sportsman's Bar, et al

the Sportsman's Bar, didn't want to sell to him because he thought Don already owned too much.

"But he put it on the market and he couldn't say no when I gave him the price he wanted," Don recalls.

By that time, Don was already an item of conversation and controversy in the community.

Getting started was not without its issues. Initially, the Village turned Don down for the transfer of the liquor license due to the disagreement over water bills in the upstairs apartments, which was still a sore subject for the Council.

"I compromised," he said. "I paid a nominal fee so they could feel like they won. There was a group of people who were dead set against anything I did."

Even so, he says, he didn't start with a preconceived idea on any of his projects, this one included.

"I saw the opportunity, I had a building business, and the buildings were cheap, so I tried to figure out what could I use them for," he says. "With the Black Sheep, here I was an instant bar owner. I had no bar knowledge; common sense prevailed, and I determined what I had to do to make things work. I'd been around long enough to know that bars are nothing more than a social center. People want to be where other people are. What was so magical about that? But it works."

He says one of the highest compliments he ever received was that about a year after he opened, a family wanted to bring their parents to the Black Sheep for their 50th anniversary.

"When you have a restaurant, you aren't selling a product — you're really selling an image," he says. "I considered what kind of places I would like to go to, and that's what I decided to create."

The name "Black Sheep" has a dual meaning, and at different times Don has used both meanings to his advantage when promoting that image. Whether it's Don's own self-description as the proverbial "black sheep" of his family, or the sheep that stands out from the crowd because of its unique color and style, each connotation benefited the Black Sheep Tavern at one time or another. Don still contends that having a name that caught people's attention was extremely important to the success of his business.

Most importantly, however, The Black Sheep Tavern that he created was a place where people could go and feel comfortable, to see and be seen. It didn't matter, he said, if beer was a nickel cheaper down the street — it was the ambiance that developed (and was continually cultivated) at the Black Sheep

If...

After:
Black Sheep Tavern

that made it among the highest-grossing restaurants in Southeastern Michigan during its heyday in the '70s.

A vaudeville-style piano player brought in people who loved to listen to him sing and play. A private wine cellar, where Don would take diners down to select their own bottle, was another drawing card. Personal service was also an added attraction.

"I had people coming from all over," Don says now. "I built the business on personal service. People would come in and see that I was there, and everything was OK. As business grew, I knocked a hole in the wall between the two buildings, got the antiques out and expanded the tavern.

But, he acknowledges, his staff was another key to his success. Don remembers a lot of good employees.

"Diane Du Russel was trained by Romanoff, who gave her a set of knives—a German tradition," remembers Don. "She was a tough taskmaster and a key person in the kitchen Diane was involved all during that period."

"My best employees came from the top third of their graduating class, and most of them never had a job before," he says.

"As high school seniors, Tim John and John Kemner were my chief cooks in the kitchen. Today, they are in business for themselves."

"I was blessed with people who were willing to work.. Wait staff never said no to another table."

Sunday afternoons were known as 'Little Europe' when beautiful and talented Lithuanians showed up to sign and play their instruments."

It was a place where people helped each other, people knew each other. "It was the original Cheers—the place where everyone knows your name," he says.

Another black sheep comes calling

"The black sheep," says Limpert, "stands out from the flock."

If...

The "Black Sheep" sign has been moved to the 115 building, but the Sportsman Bar was at 117. That was the original Sheep, and the 115 was actually Limpert's antique shop until he expanded the restaurant in 1970.

"If you can bear to hear the truth you've spoken..."

THE MILL POND APARTMENTS

When Don moved to Manchester and purchased his first building, most of the political power was centered in the office of the Chairman of the Board of the Union Savings Bank. Well-placed phone calls were usually all it took to influence any political outcome.

That power was tested when, shortly after Don's arrival in Manchester, the Council okayed the destruction of the old Davidter & Dresselhouse Hardware Building. It abutted the bank on one side and the Sportsman Tavern on the other. The urban renewal movement was in full swing and funds were available from the federal government to tear down the old and build new. The bank had plans for a drive-through window and additional parking. Don was the lone voice of opposition, not to bank improvements, but to the destruction of a Main Street building. Don lost that one.

After purchasing two more buildings adjacent to his first

If...

one, from bob Hamilton and DickWay, Don cleaned up the space behind these buildings. The bank, however, was opposed to any new buildings in that area. Don suspected they wanted it for future expansion— a suspicion confirmed later at an informal meeting in the Kopper Kettle. The Mayor and City Council refused to issue Don permits for this project.

Council's refusal to allow the apartment project led Don to acquire two vital pieces of property. Don Stockwell offered 17 acres on Duncan Street on the east side of Manchester. Next, LeRoy Marx offered the property on the river known as "the old Schaible property" which included an abandoned cemetery. This property, which a bank official had been trying to purchase for years, consisted of eight acres on the River Raisin.

Don revised his original plan for an apartment complex to fit the natural setting there along the banks of the river. He applied for a permit to build five units. The building and codes inspector, already at odds with Don over his Main Street renovations, advised Council that the sewer in that area was too small to handle any additional influx, as it was already causing backup in the Methodist Church basement. No permits were issued. A pile of used bricks that Don planned to use in construction sat on this property for the next six years.

After an election saw a new mayor take office, the sewer suddenly became adequate and Don was issued permits to build the apartments. Don chuckles at the irony of that turnaround. Part of the agreement was that Don extend the water, sewer and the paving of the road at his own expense. Don also recalls it included Council not charging tap-in fees when he hooked up those services. That part was not in writing, however, and would flare up again when he wanted to build additional units.

Mill Pond Apartments slowly took shape. Their character embraced Don's love of old brick and barn siding. Their unique style assured they were always rented by an appreciative clientele. The controversy, however, was far from over.

"Twisted by knaves to make a trap for fools..."

MANCHESTER MILL...
...a diamond in the rough

In 1981, Don performed a different kind of "rehabilitation" in the old grist mill at 201 E. Main Street in Manchester.

At the time Don bought the property from second-generation owner Ronald Mann, the mill was Michigan's longest-operating enterprise on the same site, having served the community for almost 150 years. Twice burned to the ground, the current mill was built in 1924.

Willard Mann, Ron's father, had purchased the milling business in 1940, at a time when most farmers in the area still had their grain ground into stock feed at the water-powered mill. But with modern changes in farming techniques, the mill-

If...

ing operation was no longer a financially viable part of Mann's business.

As the "milling" part of his operation began to represent a smaller and smaller fraction of Mann's business, he made the decision to move his farm and garden supply from its historic location at the hub of downtown to the west end of the village in an abandoned grocery store which he purchased from Don.

Enter Don Limpert. His original plan was to create a site for hosting large affairs such as reunions, weddings, and business gatherings at the mill, and initially had a contract with Romanoff's Catering in Ann Arbor. He shored up the deteriorating dam and mill race, created a porch from the former loading dock, decorated the interior and exterior with his signature barn lumber, and soon hosted a number of weddings and other local events.

However, when that enterprise faltered, Don, of course, had a Plan B.

As he had done so many times before, he once again reinvented the building's purpose, subdivided it, and converted the mill to accommodate small- to medium-sized retail shops. The mill quickly filled with businesses, some of whom stayed for a matter of months and others who remained for years or even decades. The longest-standing tenant of the mill is the Village Hair Forum, which has been located in the former sales wing added by the Manns in the 1970s, since shortly after Don renovated the building.

Another signature touch that Don added to the mill was living quarters. Two apartments are now located in the mill; one in the grain elevator tower and one on the lower level.

Other notable tenants in the mill have included the *Manchester Chronicle*, which ran for several years in the mid-1990s; The 18th Century Shoppe, a popular gift shop that later moved to quarters on Main Street; and Raisin Valley Antiques, a fixture in the mill for nearly 20 years. The building currently houses Worth Repeating, Inc., a charity resale shop which now encompasses most of the main floor of the mill. Today, the mill is one of Manchester's unique landmarks and is a registered Historic Site as well as being a successful business center and the venue for a variety of community oriented activities.

Karl Racenis, who with his wife, Pat, purchased the Mill from Don in 2001, says that the structural and remodeling work Don did in rehabilitating the building was "uniformly high quality." As an engineer, Racenis was extremely cautious about the prospect of purchasing a 75-year-old building along the riverfront that had served a variety of purposes over time.

"Don was very straight with us," he says. "There was noth-

If...

The mill after Don's renovation included some of his own finds and a history of the site

ing misrepresented about the condition of the building—there have been no unpleasant surprises."

Once again, Don proved that an historic building could be rehabilitated to its original beauty on the outside, while remodeling the inside to be practical and financially viable for a modern-day business.

Manchester Mill and Limpert's crew at completion of the restoration

If...

The Savannah Morning News *caught the Limperts looking over the town*

*"Or watch the things you gave your life to broker,
And stoop and build 'em up with worn out tools..."*

OTHER VENUES
Savannah to Madison

Don's love affair with Manchester waxed and waned those many years his feathered hat and broom were fixtures on Main Street. Most times his expression that Manchester was the "Center of the Universe" was heartfelt. At other times he was discouraged by the direction things took, especially in

The five-story Mill in Savannah

the political arena. Maybe there was also a restlessness to try something new, check out another opportunity, find another challenge. Whatever the reasons at play, Don did indeed find other communities in which he could practice his trademark renovation of old buildings.

Don and Rita had traveled to Savannah, Georgia on a vacation South. Both liked the town with its historic beauty and unique street layout that put most everything within walking distance. By 1972 they had sold the farm on Mahrle Road. Their youngest son, Scott, was a senior in high school, so staying put because of school was no longer required. They still owned ten buildings in Manchester, including The Black Sheep and the Mill Pond Apartments.

Rita wanted badly to leave Manchester so she spent a week in Savannah looking around. What she found was a vacant five-story former Cotton Mill. It was constructed of ballast rocks that arriving ships abandoned as they loaded cotton bales for the return trip across the ocean. It was on the river in a group of similar old buildings that an investment group had purchased to save them from the wrecking ball. This group was looking for people just like Don to renovate the structures and turn them into useful retail and restaurant type spaces. The investment group was so intent on their objective of saving these historic buildings that Don purchased the Mill with no money down. The story of the purchase even made the local papers.

Don and Rita next purchased a house in the historic downtown on Greene Square and Rita moved there. Instead of the hoped-for improvement in their relationship with the move, the marriage continued to deteriorate. Rita stayed in Savan-

If...

nah. The Mill was sold as part of the divorce settlement. Don had owned it only two years. In that time, though, he had cleaned out all five floors and made drawings of his plans for the structure. The new buyers picked up where Don left off and today the ground floor of the old Cotton Mill houses the Chart House Restaurant on the River Front.

"I came back because I owned the Black Sheep," Don recalls. "Rita never really wanted to live in Manchester."

After selling the Black Sheep in 1976, Don decided to check out some more southern areas. He headed to New Orleans. He wasn't impressed and so decided to follow the Mississippi River back to the North and visit towns along the way. He liked Cairo, Illinois, but ended up following the Ohio River and found Madison, Indiana.

Between 1976 and 1979 Don purchased six buildings in Madison on the Ohio River. This was also a city noted for appreciation of its historic past. The unique thing about Madison was that the newer part of town was out of sight of the old downtown, which made re-creating the atmosphere of the town's early years much easier. There was no unplanned jumble of old and new.

He purchased an old eight-room school, five houses and two vacant lots. Don finished renovating these properties and, in 1979, moved back to Manchester. He then started the second phase of the Mill Pond Apartments.

Contrary to popular belief, not everything Don attempted had a successful and profitable ending. In the mid-seventies he invested $20,000 to buy a half interest in the Grayling, Michigan Air Field. That sizable investment culminated with Don receiving a check for one dollar for his interest. Yes, one dollar for his investment.

Don still has that check. "You need a souvenir of your failures," he says.

*"And lose, and start again at your beginnings
And never breathe a word about your loss..."*

HARDCORE AND UNTRAINABLE
Don's own assessment of how the women in his life viewed him

Like his favorite dog, the incorrigible Ms. Dudley, Don views himself as untrainable. For the most part that's probably true. You could also add unrepentant to the list.

His first and only wife, Rita, came the closest to "reining him in" and she put up with him the longest, a true testament of her will and determination to say the least. They were married 22 years and produced two sons, Ryan and Scott. Rita, a single mother of two, met Don when he happened to walk by her house as she mowed the lawn. She blossomed in the marriage and proved to be adept at dealing with her maverick husband. Don obviously had —and still has—great respect for Rita in many ways. She was a great hostess and Don liked to have people come to visit. Even today at 80, he still has a "happy hour" at his

Rita Sneller Parry Limpert

If...

home-based tavern in Manchester.

Rita was indeed a charming and gracious hostess who could also hold her own in any discussion taking place at these gatherings. She partnered in the antique business while keeping the home fires burning and raising their four children: Ryan, Scott, Bruce, and Denise.

The next woman in Don's life was Kathy Aiuto. She started working for Don right out of high school. She was a waitress, bar maid, and eventually restaurant and Bar manager. She was protégé to Don. Kathy became astute at running a business and managing the many employees required to operate the Black Sheep Tavern.

"Kathy started working for me as a dishwasher while she was still in high school," Don recalls. "She had the ability and the aptitude; she is a natural born leader, and became my manager. The customers called her Miss Kitty, and in many ways she fit that image; she was truly a Miss Kitty. She was excellent at what she did."

Kathy Aiuto

Their business and personal relationship lasted for several years before Kathy pursued her own dream of a family and children, something Don was not prepared to do.

There were others who had perhaps best remain unidentified. Flirting with the ladies and occasionally making them blush red was as natural to Don as breathing.

Don's last major female partnership was with Flora May Neely. There is still a glint in his eye when Don recalls their first meeting. She introduced herself as "My name is Flora

May Neely...or, again, Flora May not." She was a feisty, smart woman who could more than hold her own. Their romance ended tragically when, after a day of antiquing, Flora May suffered a massive heart attack and, despite Don and the ambulance crew's best efforts, she never regained consciousness.

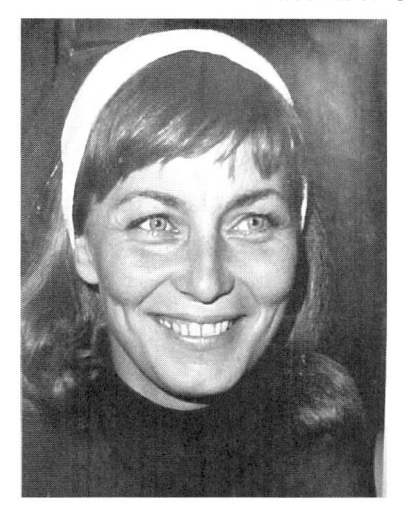

Flora May Neely

There's a lot more to be told . . . but Don doesn't want this book to become a best-seller, based on confessions.

Today, Don says he sees himself more as a mentor and listener to other people and he uses the opportunity to share his many years of experience with stories of his own.

If...

Limpert and the BIDWELL EXCHANGE BUILDING

By 1977, Don had sold the Black Sheep Tavern to brothers Christopher and Timothy Hoover and was looking for a new venture.

When Tecumseh's City Manager approached him about a vacant building downtown, it didn't take long for Don to find that venture.

The Bidwell building on the corner of Chicago Boulevard and Evans Street was named after a prominent Tecumseh family and had originally been built in 1848 as a department store, with dry goods on the street level and furniture on the second floor. The third floor had housed a Masonic Lodge and a public meeting site. At one time, it had also served as a Civil War recruiting station.

"The City Manager took me through the empty building," Don recalls. "A local family had bought it with the intention of restoring it, with money from an architectural firm in Ann Arbor. When their plans changed, they donated the building to the city as a tax write-off."

The city offered the building to Don for free, but he was characteristically suspicious of such an offer.

"I realize there's no such thing as 'free,'" he notes. "I learned that there was $9,000 in outstanding taxes so I offered $10,000. The city council was very happy with the deal."

One contingency of the sale was that the building not be torn down, but rather restored and made useable within 180 days.

When Don bought it, the original Bidwell building had been subdivided into three sections. He bought two of the three to renovate into retail shops. The third was a bar at that time. The bar was eventually purchased by an attorney, who spruced it up to match Don's "Bidwell Exchange" restoration.

Even before the building was ready, the building had a full roster of seven tenants lined up, including an antique store (of course), a salon, a health food store and a second-floor dance studio.

"On the 180th day, we had a ribbon cutting," Don says. "I was running a couple of minutes late, so I quickly found a parking place and went to the ceremony. It lasted about 10 minutes and I returned to find a ticket on my car."

So much for the appreciation of a community. During his years as a building owner in Tecumseh, Don was instrumental in getting the parking meters removed from the downtown area and promoting off-street parking behind the buildings.

"Parking is always critical to a business," he says. "A lot of people still don't get that."

After four or five years of ownership, Don found a buyer who has carried on in the same tradition, with the building still remaining a viable retail site more than 25 years later.

If...

Circa 1900 Schneider Blacksmith Shop

*"And so hold on when there is nothing in you
Except the Will which says to them: 'Hold on'..."*

BLACKSMITH SHOP

Many historic buildings have been saved by the simple failure of the owners to upgrade and modernize them. They sit neglected for decades, aging and forgotten. Many of these old structures will eventually get torn down when the real estate on which they sit becomes more valuable than the building itself.

A few lucky old buildings are purchased by people like Don Limpert who once again bring them back to life and usefulness. Such a lucky building was Manchester's John Schneider Blacksmith Shop on Main Street.

Owned by the Schneider family estate which consisted of three daughters, the building was offered for sale in 1977. Don happened to be back in town checking on his other properties when he learned it was for sale. He was still involved with his project in Madison, Indiana. As with all Don's other real estate purchases, he looked at the building and within an hour had borrowed the amount on a personal note and made a full-price cash offer. Ever the shrewd businessman, Don knew it was the only way he could purchase the property. One of the daughters was not a fan of Don's, to put it mildly.

The Historical Society had also been looking and talking about the property for some time. It was the organization's hope that a benefactor would purchase it and donate it to them.

The building dates to 1877, built by a Civil War veteran who lived across the street. A buggy factory was housed in a frame building next door. According to Don there were only three previous owners prior to his purchase, the last owner being the Schneiders. There were originally three forges. Two had been taken out as the blacksmith business changed from a horse-oriented one to other metal working including making the rims for converting older farm machinery and tractors to rubber tires.

In the twenty or more years since it ceased to be an operating business, the building had been used by Schneider's son-in-law L.V. Kirk. "It was full of junk," Don recalls and he didn't mean valuable antiques. The windows had all been covered with metal sheeting and Don's first task was remov-

If...

1946 John Schneider   *The Blacksmith Shop in 2009*

ing the metal and getting natural light back into the building.

The forge was badly in need of repair and even some of the foundation brick had to be replaced. Don had purchased it "as is." There had also been other modifications to the structure over the years, but Don restored it to its original state. He put in a bathroom. (That brought laughter as Don recalled the "bathroom" at the Mann's Feed Mill downtown which he also purchased and restored. That "restroom facility" consisted of a "funnel" located part way down the basement stairs with a rubber tube leading to the mill race.)

He also installed central heat and air conditioning and all new electrical service. It took extensive labor on Don's part to restore the structure to what can be seen today.

In 1983 the Manchester Historical Society approached Don about purchasing the building. Don agreed to sell it for exactly his out-of-pocket expense: his original $15,000 plus $7,500 in materials, heat, electric, etc. Don donated his extensive labor in restoring the building. He also donated all the blackmith tools valued at about $3500, some original to the building, others acquired. Don later became president of the Society and is still today an active member of the Board.

Macomber & Chartrand
MANCHESTER HAD CHANGED

A real estate poster from about 1976

If...

Looking west, Michigan Avenue, Clinton, Michigan, 1930s post card

*"If you can force your heart and nerve and sinew
To serve your turn long after they are gone..."*

THE CLINTON HOTEL

Henry Ford frequently stayed at the old Clinton Inn coach stop (circa 1832) and liked it so much that he bought it, tore it down, and reassembled it in his Greenfield Village complex in Dearborn, Michigan.

Just a few doors west of that empty lot, Don Limpert liked the Clinton Hotel even more—so much so that he restored the aging structure and left it where it was—in the heart of downtown Clinton, Michigan.

Don's purchase of the Clinton Hotel in 1986 started as many of his previous projects had: he was sought out by the then-current owner.

The historic three-story hotel, built in 1901, included three adjacent buildings and was at the time suffering from a rather seedy reputation with cheap rooms and apartments rented by the week to a less than stellar clientele. The establishment also included a dining room and bar, but at the time they were not very functional.

There was no way Don could make the needed improve-

South façade of the restored Clintonian Inn

ments with the rooms occupied, so he cleared the building and started renovations.

This time, he had the blessing of the Village fathers, in part because they were anxious to rid the downtown of that particular clientele and they anticipated something similar to the Black Sheep Tavern Don had created in Manchester.

When Don and his crew finished some "pretty major renovations" of the building, the hotel included 12 overnight rooms and four apartments. He had successfully restored the building to what had been a state-of-the-art local hotel in the early 1900s. A Drummer's Room, where peddlers would gather to display their wares, is now the tavern. Don expanded the dining room by cutting through a wall into the next building, which had been a retail store.

Unlike his early difficulties in Manchester with Village officials, Don found Clinton highly supportive of his efforts. At Don's suggestion and urging, they started cleaning up the backs of the buildings and creating additional parking. And, as is usually the case, other building owners started following Don's example by fixing up their own store fronts. A couple of other building owners even hired Don to do the work.

Don sold his house on Main Street in Manchester around

If...

West and east dining rooms of the Clintonian Inn

this time and purchased one in Adrian. He mostly lived there while he was working on his projects in Clinton and Tecumseh.

Though the hotel was moderately successful and certainly a vast improvement from its recent past, Don's and the community's dream of another Black Sheep Tavern success story did not happen. Don tried to capitalize on his experience from the

Artist Bill Shurtliff's painting of the rehabilitated Clontonian Inn, 1986

Black Sheep, but unlike back in Manchester, he could not assemble the creative and loyal team it took to make the venture a success. He had to rely totally on hired help to run the hotel, restaurant, and bar and, for whatever reason, he could not put together the same caliber of help to do so.

Today, Don recalls it as a successful venture, but not a profitable one. He sold the Clinton Hotel in 1991 to Mark and Laurie Pedersen, who still own it today. Mark Pedersen was a trained chef and hotel manager who traveled extensively for a major hotel chain. As the couple's family grew, he sought a way to be able to stay closer to home and have a business of his own. The Clinton Inn was the perfect solution for the young family, and Don considers the business they have built as a credit to the community. His satisfaction lies in the fact that it is still a viable and integral part of Clinton's downtown and is doing well.

Meanwhile, he had purchased a 40-acre farm off M-52 back in Manchester. He also acquired additional land nearby and once again the sounds of chickens and geese echoed on the Limpert property. In 1998, the property was sold to a local developer and eventually re-zoned for industrial use.

If...

At age 85, Manchester Enterprise founder and long-time owner, Mat Blosser still fed his hand press at the Enterprise office.

*"If neither foes nor loving friends can hurt you;
If all men count with you, but none too much..."*

DON AND *THE ENTERPRISE* (aka Limpert & Garlick)

Don had what might be termed a "devil's alliance" relationship with Emory Garlick, another man seen as somewhat of a renegade to Old Manchester.

Like Limpert, Garlick was an outsider who came to Manchester by chance. He grew up in Wayne, and spent a good share of his summers on the family farm not far from the little hamlet of Willis. As a teen during World War II, he often would accompany his uncle to Manchester where they would pick up eggs from his aunt, Ann Garlick Fuller, who lived on the west side of town, to be later delivered in Ypsilanti and Melvindale. Her husband Densel Fuller worked for Dresselhouse and Davidter, in the implement store that occupied the area between Comerica Bank and the building that later housed the Black Sheep Tavern.

"On occasion, we would stop and warm ourselves by the round bellied stove in the store," he recalls. "The Haller's had the meat market; there was a 5 & 10 cent store and other buildings on Main Street. Manchester during those days was a viable community with many small businesses."

About 1973 Garlick, by now a Civil Engineer, bought the land on which the Deutschgrat Subdivision is now located, the same land that was previously owned by his uncle, Densel Fuller. His children both graduated from Manchester High School and the family was active at Emanuel United Church of Christ.

"During this period of time I would on occasion stop at the coffee shop and we would occasionally dine at the Black Sheep Tavern to accumulate slivers from the rustic furniture," he recalls. "The ambience was primitive to say the least. I became acquainted with both the Village Council and Manchester Township Board during the period when developing the property. I found all of the members most cooperative and enthusiastic in having a new development. Don and I struck up a conversation of the intricacies of small town politics."

"I became aware of some of the old power players at Union Savings Bank," Emory added. "During this time frame the power infighting over control of the bank reached its zenith. Both sides thought that manipulation and deal making was the road to success and power, and intimidation was the by-word of both factions."

Don and Emory may have shared a deep disdain for some of those same "power players," whether in the bank or the governmental structure of the village and surrounding townships, but they certainly were not on the same side of every issue in local politics.

In 1982 or 83, Manchester Township Supervisor Clarence Fielder contacted Garlick to become the building inspector for Manchester, Bridgewater and Freedom Townships as well as the Village of Manchester. As a Michigan Registered Civil Engineer, builder and contractor, Emory had both the training and experience to offer the position. Since Don had done

If...

so much building and remodeling work during the 1960s and 1970s, many of the inspections for which Emory was called upon involved buildings that Don had built and subsequently sold.

"Remodeling found some structural inadequacies that did not conform to new codes," he says. A lot of the materials used were reclaimed lumber both for structural work and interior finish. Typically, for the time of construction, minimal materials were used that no longer conformed to new codes. The interior trim work, in particular the unfinished barn wood and open brick work, ran Don afoul of the Washtenaw County Health Department. During my tenure Don was not building and was doing only minimal trim work."

In the mid-1980s, Garlick sold his company, built a new home in Manchester, and continued as building inspector. As Village Council debated the advantages of Manchester Plastics' addition to their current facility on wetlands that backed up to Garlick's Deutschgrat subdivision, Garlick objected strenuously and was removed from inspection duties for the plant.

"*The Manchester Enterprise*, then owned by Simon Steele, dutifully published my position (in letters to the editor) but refused to become involved," Garlick said. "Limpert shared my position but the power structure was such that no one listened. Don and I thought that a newspaper that responded to legitimate concerns was needed in Manchester and thus the seed was placed in our minds."

Don was on council at that time and a new Village Manager was hired. When the manager ran afoul of Council and was terminated, Don proposed Emory as the interim Village Manager.

"Within a few months Village business settled; staff picked up the slack and I stepped down," Garlick says. "I stepped on a few toes I'm sure as owning my own business for so many years did not bode well for government interaction, and I might add Don resigned during that period of time for the same reasons I believe. Don and I would commiserate about the political infighting."

Meanwhile, the "Emptyprise" as Don and Emory coined it, reported little if anything that could be termed news during the last few years of Steele's ownership. The two would spend evenings talking over dinner of the inadequacies they perceived at the paper. Don was mostly concerned with the local government issues, while Emory had major concerns with the school system.

Mat Blosser at his Enterprise *desk, early 1900s*

"One evening over our meal and libations we proposed buying that 'rag,' but the only problem was how to operate the paper," Emory recalls. "Don was adamant about not being involved with the operation of the paper but was willing to provide information about government functions. We proposed equal partners in the investment with me overseeing day to day operation. We bought the paper from Simon and hired Janet Shurtliff as the Editor/Publisher. Janet to her credit was instrumental in revamping the paper. Don wanted one thing included under the masthead, 'The Center of the Universe,' and with that we were in motion."

This was in late 1991. After several months, Garlick bought Limpert's initial investment and assumed control of the paper.

Don had an uncanny ability to ferret out information on individuals and their interaction with Manchester's governmental bodies. He was always on the alert for what he termed hanky-panky. He loved to use the saying, "The steam that blows the whistle doesn't turn the wheel," and occasionally that fit the circumstances of the politicos. Don also had an inherent distrust of individuals who fed from the trough of public financing through their association with Council and other bodies.

Although Don was not particularly interested in the school

If...

system, he was always willing to give Emory his take on the issues, including ideas for the old middle school building that could have been a significant addition to the community. Unfortunately, nothing would develop from those ideas.

Garlick, too, eased out of his association with the newspaper by selling the Enterprise to his partner and she was eventually bought out by the Heritage Newspapers chain.

Don still has a framed copy of the first issue of The Enterprise *published by Limpert & Garrick*

"So ended Don's and my input," he says. "We had a great deal of fun and I felt that we accomplished a lot with the help of many, many people. In 2003, I moved to Texas, but I stop to see Don when in town and he fills me in on a lot of the crap going on."

*"If you can talk with crowds and keep your virtue,
Or walk with kings - nor lose the common touch..."*

CENTER OF THE UNIVERSE
Don's vision and views

When Don Limpert and Emory Garlick purchased *The Manchester Enterprise*, Don's one insistence was that the banner atop the front page read "The Center of the Universe." In many ways, this summarizes Don's relationship with his adopted community.

Those who agree with Don and those who disagree vehemently must all agree on one thing: Don Limpert has indelibly changed the face of Manchester since his arrival here in 1963. He has taken on bankers and lawyers; government officials and newspaper editors; and he very nearly single-handedly changed this small, "ghost town" village into a thriving community.

Local businessman and Downtown Development Authority Chair Karl Racenis has known Don since he purchased the Mill from him in 2001. Racenis says that he and Don may occasionally have their differences of opinion, but they usually agree more than they disagree.

"We like to debate the issues, however," he says with a chuckle. "And I always say that debating with an engineer is like mud wrestling with a pig—everyone gets dirty and the pig enjoys it."

The same could probably be said for debating with Don Limpert.

"One thing I have always appreciated about Don," Racenis continues, "is that he is really the only person I've ever encountered who puts his money where his mouth is when it comes to historic preservation. Not many entrepreneurs would do that—and that is how Don is different from most entrepreneurs."

If...

Don has always put his money where his mouth is in any argument. When he believed that the important conversations were not taking place in the newspaper, he bought it and made it the center of his universe. Today, the "center of the universe" is around Don's table at his self-styled tavern in his home in the southeast corner of the village of Manchester. The site is reminiscent of the Black Sheep Tavern at its best.

"This is where the important conversations take place in this community," he has told me. I've yet to discover that for myself, but I have no doubt that it is true.

Don is the product of a unique set of values that no longer really exists today. He says he's a relic; the last of a breed—a person who values common sense above all else.

"Whatever happened to self-reliance, hard work and common sense?" he asks. "The entrepreneur doesn't do things alone any more; he is always looking for a handout. The day of the true entrepreneur is gone. We have overregulated ourselves; fairness and common sense have all but disappeared."

Of Manchester's "kingpins" in the '60s, Don says he has outlived most of them. And he beat them at their own game by taking a few risks. "I had more guts than money; that was my advantage," he says today.

Don proudly states that he has been at odds with the governmental bodies of the community for over 45 years. Whether it was a water bill or development plan, he continued to fight—and he's often won. And of the times that he hasn't, he is philosophical. After all, he's still here and kicking.

"It's not personal, it's not emotional," he says. "It's a little late for me to start over, but I'm trying to pass on what I've learned. This community needs to get an open mind—they need to get their heads out of the sand. They don't have a plan."

When Don moved here, the Union Savings Bank powers were hell-bent on urban renewal. They succeeded in tearing down the Dresselhouse-Davidter Hardware, but Don single-handedly saved many more buildings on Main Street that could have been similarly doomed, by purchasing and rehabilitating them.

The key feature of "rehabilitation" versus renovation or restoration is that in rehabilitating Manchester's old buildings, Don retained and preserved their essential architectural and historic charm, but made them usable in a current context. He created small office spaces where there had been large mercantile stores that no longer had a purpose in the current economy. He created a museum, restored an historic blacksmith forge and meeting place out of what had been a storage barn for many years. He built apartments on the upper levels of buildings that had remained unused for decades. And he created viable retail space on a 150-year-old feed mill site.

"I kind of created a monster," he acknowledges. "Now, everyone is talking about preservation, but how are they going to preserve it? They need to be competitive, and make this town into a destination."

That's what Don did in the '70s with the Black Sheep Tavern. The Black Sheep was a typical small-town farmer's saloon in 1968 when it was known as the Sportsman's Bar. Within a few years, it became a region-wide beacon attracting people from all over the state to downtown Manchester.

Today, he says, another gift shop, or new trees and park benches as planned by the current Downtown Development Authority, are not going to create that kind of a destination. A plan for attracting viable businesses to downtown Manchester is what Don believes is needed to preserve the small community atmosphere that has come to be valued. Manchester's uniqueness is due in great deal to what Don has created and what he envisioned 45 years ago. He had a plan, and he carried it out—at least where he was able.

"What I've done, I could never do again today," he says. "No one can—there is too much overregulation and no real goals. My support came from the silent majority and that is what helped me be successful.

"Everybody thinks people aren't interested—that they don't care. I'm convinced the vast majority do care. Many times they don't even realize it. When an issue comes up, whatever it is, they may not say a word but they care. That's the

If...

silent majority. Give them a reason; they will care. That's my way of explaining it and that surely was the support I had. It helped me stand up against the good old boys network."

Don is not happy with Manchester's current political situation, with what he sees as the local governmental units (Manchester village and its surrounding townships) giving up local control. He remains critical of those governmental officials today who would hire outsiders and "professionals" with a college degree to help the community make progress on theory. He also views the Village and Manchester Township as two "kingdoms" within a square mile that don't communicate effectively and says that this lack of working together will end up relinquishing local control of land use.

"We need to have more uneducated positive thinkers," he says. "Education tends to get in the way of common sense. I would never hire a college graduate; I didn't want to have to retrain them."

While no one could claim to do or attempt to do exactly what Don did starting 45 years ago in Manchester, in this time of economic instability lie the seeds of opportunity and the possibility of a newer Manchester emerging. The real story here, Don insists, is not a story about an individual, but rather about a philosophy. It's about the opportunities that are out there, no matter who you are. And he is prepared to let history judge what he's done and come to their own conclusions.

"That's the message I'd like to convey, mostly by example. I may have initiated it; I did a lot of the up front things, but I didn't do it with the help of the establishment.

"I've been here so long, now I'm an insider; or at least I've outlived all my enemies. You can never be a judge of yourself; your best judge is the people who surround you."

*"If you can fill the unforgiving minute
With sixty seconds' worth of distance run…"*

A COMMITMENT TO MANCHESTER'S HISTORY

With a long record of making history, Don Limpert made it again in 2004, as the Washtenaw County Historic District Commission named him the lone individual recipient of its Historic Preservation Award for his unique preservation efforts of Manchester's commercial district over the past 40 years.

The awards were established in 2003 to honor individuals who have furthered preservation efforts in Washtenaw County.

"Don was actually ahead of the historic preservation movement, which started in the 1970s," said Marnie Paulus, the county's historic preservation coordinator. "He was very forward thinking and he put his own resources on the line.

"Most recently, his work on the Manchester Mill was a good rehabilitation project, making sure that the character was not lost while creating an effective reuse project inside the building."

Paulus, in an *Ann Arbor News* article published at the time of his award, described Don as a "visionary" and added that Manchester's welcoming downtown area is due largely to his influence.

Don was nominated for the 2004 award by Manchester resi-

If...

dents Karl Racenis and Larry Byrne.

"Don chose to invest in his rehabilitation plan and purchased 10 historic buildings on Main Street," according to their nomination letter. "He used his learned skills as a journeyman carpenter and building designer, combined with his love of history, and began the revitalization of Manchester's downtown district."

When Don came to Manchester with his family in the early 1960s he had the specific intent of "rehabilitating" its downtown area. He saw the potential in the downtown's 19th-century Italianate buildings and labored tirelessly to restore and preserve the character of the community.

Don is a charter member of the Civil War Historical Association dedicated to preserving history of the post-war era.

During the first week of every August, Don reasserts his membership in the Breweriana Collectors, with special interests in history and beer making.

He has been involved with planning and zoning since the late '60s and served as chair of the Township Planning Commission.

He continues that dedication at 82, recently concluding a second term on the Manchester Village Planning Commission, a seat he's held since 2003, after serving for two years in the 1980s. He has also served as a village trustee (1986-87), the chair of the Historic District Study Commission (2004-05), Manchester Township planning commissioner. And his commitment to preserving history is evident in his membership in the Manchester Area Historical Society since 1984, including a five-year term as president from 2001-2006. He's also a member of the Ann Arbor and Adrian Historical Societies and the Historical Society of Michigan.

"Those that opposed his restoration plan in favor of urban renewal found Don to be a worthy opponent," concludes Racenis and Byrne's 2004 nomination letter. "… And, some may still say, very hard-headed."

*"Yours is the Earth and everything that's in it,
And - which is more - you'll be a Man my son!"*

LIMPERT IS NOMINATED

Dear Awards Committee: February 11, 2006
We are writing to you in regards to your quest to honor an individual who through personal effort and involvement in historic preservation projects made a significant contribution to the preservation of Michigan's heritage.

Mr. Donald E. Limpert moved his family to the Village of Manchester during the 1960's. He chose Manchester to be his home for mainly one reason; his vision to "rehabilitate" the downtown. He believed renovation works for museums, but historical buildings must be rehabilitated to their original beauty on the outside, while remodeling the inside to be practical and financially viable for current businesses.

In one sense his timing couldn't have been worse. The 1960's, as you know, were a time for "Urban Renewal" and all communities, large and small, were tearing down historical buildings due to many inefficiencies and putting up steel and glass boxes. This too was the situation that owners of the Manchester's downtown Italianate buildings had to acknowledge. At that time many of the buildings were empty and most were in dire need of restoration. Mr. Limpert chose to invest in his rehabilitation plan and purchased ten of the historical buildings on Main Street. He used his learned skills as a journeyman carpenter and building designer combined with his love of history and began the revitalization of Manchester's downtown district. Those that opposed his restoration plan in favor of urban renewal found Mr. Limpert to be a worthy opponent and as some may still say "Very

If...

Hard Headed." He has a passion for history, especially the Civil War era. It is said that he has one of the best private collections of Civil War memorabilia in the country. The Manchester Blacksmith shop on East Main Street was another one of Mr. Limpert's rehabilitation projects. Afterward, he sold the building to the local historical society at cost and donated the contents. It is believed to be the oldest operating Blacksmith Shop in Michigan and is now home to the Manchester Area Historical Society.

Currently seventy eight years young, Mr. Limpert has participated in community planning and historic preservation for many years and is currently an active member of the Manchester Village Planning Commission. The historic village of Manchester is a small jewel in the crown of the State of Michigan. We hope this information together with the attached photographs and CD files will promote Mr. Donald E. Limpert for your 2006 Citizen Award.

Respectfully submitted by:
    Larry E. Byrne   Karl I. Racenis

from Mlive.com
Everything Michigan

Manchester man keeps history alive. Don Limpert's lifelong passion has been the preservation, renovation of buildings

Saturday, 3, 2004
BY LISA KLIONSKY News Staff Reporter

Step into Don Limpert's "pub" in his Manchester home, as his friends often do late in the afternoon and glimpse into his past, into the days when he owned and ran the well-known Black Sheep Tavern.

There's a long wooden bar with glass jars filled with salty snacks, stained glass light fixtures, and plenty of mugs, chair and round tables.

In the annex to his home, Limpert keeps a Civil War memorabilia collection; articles that include a chair that President Lincoln may have sat from the Illinois state Legislature, Civil War uniforms, nurse Clara Barton's first Missing in Action lsit an letters form confederate and union soldiers to their families.

Limpert, 77, loves history and he lives his passion. A carpenter and entrepreneur, his life's work has been to purchase, restore and resell buildings not just in Manchester but also in Tecumseh and Clinton, and in Savannah, Ga, and Madison, Ind.

He's recently been recognized by Washtenaw County with a historic preservation award for his work on more than a dozen Manchester buildings.

County officials credit him with preserving the character of the original 19th –century Italianate commercial district and giving the community an "enlivened social and economic center." They gave him special recognition for his ongoing quest to rehabilitate the Manchester Mill, which is listed on the State Register of Historic Places.

Limpert's vision for Manchester, located west of Ann Arbor, began as early s the mid-1960s and has never wavered.

"His efforts kept Manchester's downtown buildings from being torn down . . . He rehabilitated buildings so they'd maintain their historic charm and be usable," said Karl Racenis, Manchester's planning commission chair.

Limpert "has always been a history lover… His specialty was to rehabilitate and restore old builds. … Instead of trying to restore them to be historically accurate, his view was to… *ad infinitum*

If...

Limpert is aggrandized in the Jackson Citizen-Patriot

'REHABILITATION' IS KEY TO MANCHESTER'S PAST

By Robert Curamins, Ann Arbor News Staff Reproter
Sunday, November 10, 1974

A man who believes that the small town is "the last frontier of Americana" is putting his theories to the test in Manchester.

His name is Don Limpert and he describes himself as a "building rehabilitator."

His hope is that Manchester will look more and more like a turn-of-the-century village while blending and harmonizing old and new and avoiding entirely the neon-jungle look of most areas.

During the last few years, Limpert has bought eight buildings on Manchester's Main Street. The facades have been restored where necessary, brick-work refurbished, paint applied, neat and modest signs hung above business places, ornamental ironwork used where appropriate—all in keeping with the idea of maintaining "a working connection with the past."

The Black Sheep Tavern, owned by Limpert, is one of his first and best known projects. Known for many years as the Sloat Bros. Saloon, it had long been, says Limpert, "a typical small-town saloon where farmers and businessmen played cards and talked about crops.

In the last five years, while expanding to an adjacent building and a lower level, Limpert has "rehabilitated" the tavern into his own image of what it should be—a blend of old and new which can serve as a social center.

One of the most striking facts is that he has used predominantly the materials and mementos of the past that he found right there in the old building—wood, bricks, old tables, bottles, decanters, signs and so on.

He takes us on a tour.

"The first thing I did was to expose the brick walls by removing the old plaster," he said. "The beams and other wood from the dining room came from the old Michigan Central depot, which was torn down in 1965.

"The bar in the Black Sheep Tavern was made by hand in 1886," Limpert says. "I doubt it was originally at this location. There were seven taverns in town at one time, and it probably moved around."

Here is a sign from 1880 for Grove Brewery. "The Brewery was on Grove Street in Ypsilanti," Limpert explains. Another sign, for Paul Jones whisky, depicts a happy senior citizen above the legend, "Comrades for 81 years."

Framed and hung on the wall is an ad for a dance to be held at the Saline Opera House with music by the Michigan Melody Men from the U-M. Another frame contains a collection of early receipts for land purchases in Michigan. They bear the dates of 1835 and 1837.

We go down to the basement and Limpert points out

If...

something unusual about the bricks; many of them contain fingerprints. "The bricks were made locally and some were just handled before they had hardened," says Limpert. "Some of them have chicken tracks in them or the print of a cat's paw. These bricks came from an oven that used to be in the basement.

Many of the tables are the original tavern tables. "You can tell by the shelf underneath, " Limpert explains. "The customer put his beer on the shelf while he played cards on the top."

Here is a cistern covered by an old cast-iron floor register. Limpert calls it "the biggest ash tray in the state of Michigan."

Limpert says he looked around for a year and half before he settled on Manchester as the place to test his theory.

He chose the village because "it was off the main road, and virtually untouched by a commercial and business influx. There was no uncontrolled or low-standard growth. It was ideally located in the heart of an area containing six or seven million people. And it had a high percentage of vacant buildings on Main Street."

Since then Limpert has acquired eight of those Main Street buildings. One of them is next door and is occupied by a branch of Ann Arbor Savings and Loan. We see that here too the bricks have been exposed. "The wood used here is barn wood," Limpert tells us. Beyond that is an office building rehabilitated in the same way.

"Look on Main Street," says Limpert. "You see no neon signs and more than 50 percent of the façades are in their original state or rehabilitated."

Limpert likes the word "rehabilitate," in preference to "renovate" or "restore" because he believes in combining the new with the old in harmonious ways.

The village fathers agree with him, he says, on adopting the image of a turn-of-the-century village. "Now that we have agreement on that," he says, "the next thing is to implement the zoning rules on façades, signs, and destruction of buildings."

The rear of the buildings are just as important as the front, Limpert maintains. He takes us to the rear of the tavern-bank-office group. Stairs and balconies with ornamental iron work have been built as entrances to apartments on the second floor. A wild grape vine twists it way along a balcony. "Old sheds and undergrowth were removed to make way for parking," Limpert says.

"Many communities don't allow living above business places," he continues, "but that's what these buildings were designed for."

We get into a pickup truck for a ride to see more apartments, built on a tract overlooking the River Raisin. Limpert follows a dirt road on an old railroad right of way until we come to a hilltop.

"This land was like a jungle when I bought it. It turned out to be an old burial ground. It had been vandalized long ago and its headstones were scattered about." Limpert intends to use most of it as the site of future apartments maintaining the rest of the old burial ground as a private park.

Some apartments have already been built overlooking the river. Again we see the motifs of brick and barn wood. And Limpert gives us more of his philosophy. "Meet the demand, but don't overbuild. That's the healthy way of growing. Don't reject the new. Mix old and new. Make them blend and harmonize."

Although Limpert and Manchester were new to each other until a few years ago, he comes from "an old Washtenaw County family." They came from Germany to Freedom Township in 1834," he says. "Then they moved into Ann Arbor. My grandfather was a jeweler in Ann Arbor for over 50 years."

Limpert is a believer in Manchester.

"It has some great natural assets, including the river. There is a balance here between the rural and the suburban. It is not just a bedroom community, nor is it an old town that refuses to change. In a community of only 1,800 people, there are 700 jobs. And the people have pride."

If...

Limpert says others in town besides himself are "rehabilitating." As we ride along, he points to a long-time church as an example. It now contains offices. We pass a former blacksmith shop on Main Street. "Something could be done with that," he notes.

Obviously, Liimpert believes he chose well when he made Manchester "the last frontier" in his battle for Americana.

"We don't gain national identity by destroying our past," were his parting words.

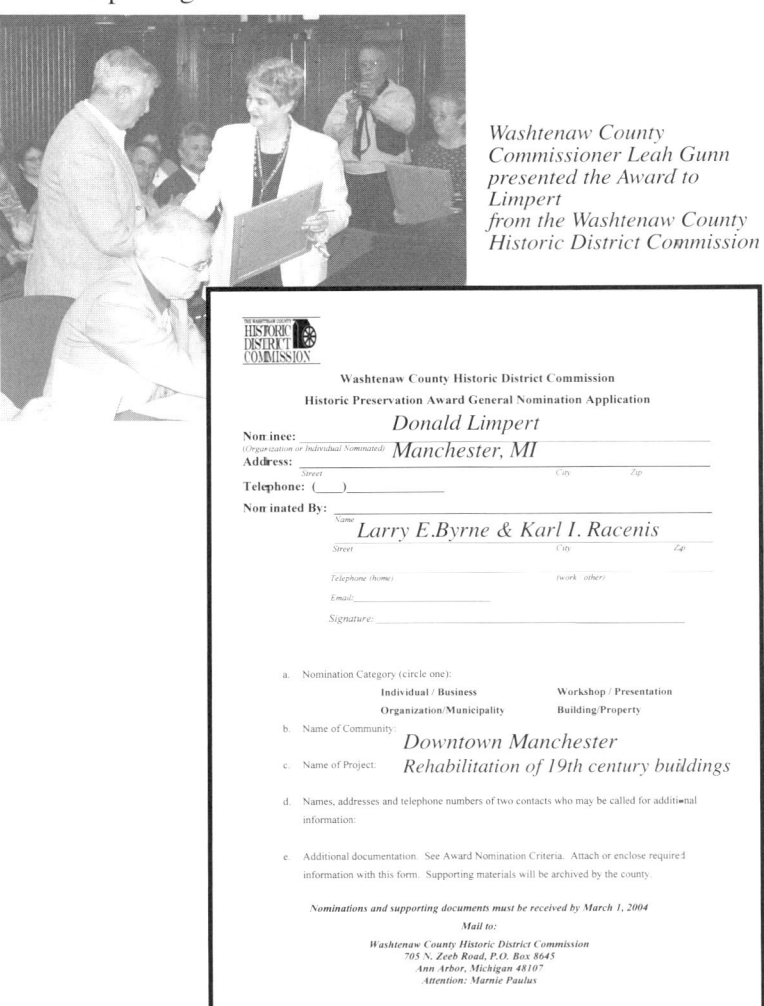

Washtenaw County Commissioner Leah Gunn presented the Award to Limpert from the Washtenaw County Historic District Commission

---

Washtenaw County Historic District Commission
Historic Preservation Award General Nomination Application

Nominee: *Donald Limpert*
(Organization or Individual Nominated)
Address: *Manchester, MI*
  Street   City   Zip
Telephone: (   )
Nominated By:
  Name: *Larry E. Byrne & Karl I. Racenis*
  Street   City   Zip
  Telephone (home):   (work/other):
  Email:
  Signature:

a. Nomination Category (circle one):
   Individual / Business   Workshop / Presentation
   Organization/Municipality   Building/Property
b. Name of Community: *Downtown Manchester*
c. Name of Project: *Rehabilitation of 19th century buildings*
d. Names, addresses and telephone numbers of two contacts who may be called for additional information:
e. Additional documentation. See Award Nomination Criteria. Attach or enclose required information with this form. Supporting materials will be archived by the county.

Nominations and supporting documents must be received by March 1, 2004
Mail to:
Washtenaw County Historic District Commission
705 N. Zeeb Road, P.O. Box 8645
Ann Arbor, Michigan 48107
Attention: Marnie Paulus

CIVIL WAR COLLECTION

When viewing Don's success at most every endeavor he attempts, one would assume he thinks out everything methodically in advance. Not true. Most of his real estate purchases, for instance, including those on Main Street in Manchester, were spur-of-the-moment decisions. "Buy it first," he grins, "then figure out what to do with it." His Civil War collection is a similar case in point.

Part of his duties as a young man were cleaning and painting his father's apartments. When one became empty, Don would get it ready to be rented again. He was in his early teens cleaning up one such apartment when he came across an old leather duffle bag that had been left behind. Inside were letters, ribbons, and a diary of a Civil War veteran. Instead of throwing it away, Don took it home and began reading the contents. It turns out the veteran had only recently died and had been a dentist like Don's father.

Thus began a lifelong involvement in Civil War memorabilia. It peaked during the centennial celebration in 1961 to '65. He became a reenactor and with his sons, Ryan and Scott and

If...

Top: A corner of Limpert's living room. Center: President Lincoln's chair
Bottom: Todd Lincoln with father Abraham in the chair

brother Frank, they participated in many parades and reenactments around the country. Don also organized the Civil War re-enactment that took place in Manchester for its 100-year celebration in 1967.

His collection today is quite extensive including a chair that was purchased by Matthew Brady for a studio prop. It was originally a fixture in the House of Representatives ca. 1859. A famous photo of Lincoln and his son, with Lincoln sitting in this chair, was taken by Brady during his presidency. Don has some of the more popular things like guns and uniforms, but much of his collection consists of memorabilia from the veterans' groups formed after the War, namely the Grand Army of the Republic (GAR) and United Confederate Veterans (UCV). Don has also gathered information on many of the veterans from Michigan and tries to put a history to as much of his collection as possible.

Grand Army of the Republic emblem

Don's own ancestors, who moved from Germany to Scio Township in 1834, did not fight directly in the war.

Since no one else in his family has Don's interest in his collection, he is selling it to other collectors. For a while Don looked into other options including buying a building in Gettysburg, Pennsylvania and opening a museum. Another option was donating it to the collection of the National Trust for Historic Preservation. In every case the labor involved—and the uncertainty of how others would display and care for the collection—caused Don to finally decide that other collectors should have a chance to purchase it. If they pay for it, he reasons, they're more likely to take good care of it.

An abandoned leather bag led to a lifetime love of Civil War artifacts. Much of Don's collection would have ended up thrown away and lost forever since personal mementoes like the ribbons won in battle are not viewed as being as valuable as the more popular objects like guns and uniforms. It seems renovating and saving old buildings was not Don's only contribution to the preservation of our country's past. Remembering and saving mementoes of the Civil War veterans is also Don's legacy.

If...

That's Rudy, at right, hard at work as usual

RUDY LORIN:
Friend and Fellow Carpenter

One man who could have no doubt filled many pages of this book with stories about Don was long time friend and carpenter, Rudy Lorin. Don's great respect for Rudy shows in how he describes their working together for over twenty-five years. Don used the words, "with me" in describing Rudy's help on such projects as the Spiegel Stores, Don's personal house on Mahrle Road, and the Mill Pond Apartments in Manchester. There were all Don's projects. He was the boss, as such, but in Don's eyes they were simply two talented carpenters working together. On many projects, Don's brother Fred also joined in.

Don recalls fondly that he and Rudy had many great times together. Back in those early years they both smoked cigars. According to Don, both smoked a box of 50 each week.

Rudy was a World War Two veteran who had been captured by the Germans in the Battle of the Bulge. A lifelong carpenter, Rudy's last project with Don was a dental office for a Dr. Burk in 1975...or so he thought! Don later talked Rudy out of retirement to help with the Baurenstube Bar/Restaurant in Manchester. They renovated two buildings near the River Raisin for owner, Bob Lawson.

OPEN HOUSE
Celebrates Limpert's 80th Birthday

By Ed Patino, Staff Writer,
The Manchester Enterprise
PUBLISHED: May 3, 2007
Four decades ago, Don Limpert made a commitment to preserve the heritage of downtown Manchester.

The village will have the chance to further show its gratitude for him Sunday. An open house to celebrate Limpert's 80th birthday will take place from 3 to 7 p.m. Sunday at the River Ridge Clubhouse.

Limpert is perhaps best known for his actions in the 1960s that helped Manchester preserve its old-time charm. During a decade of "modernization," developers were looking at purchasing buildings in the business district to give the town a more modern look. Limpert purchased several downtown buildings, including The Mill ... to prevent the developers from "modernizing" the area.

"Don owned about 13 buildings," Manchester Village President Pat Vailliencourt said. "We owe Don a great amount of gratitude for protecting the heritage of downtown Manchester."

Even at 80 years young, Limpert remains active with the Manchester Historical Society. Along with preserving the town's heritage, Limpert preserves items celebrating the country's history.

"He has a Civil War collection that can compete with anything you see at museums across the nation," Vailliencourt said.

The River Ridge Clubhouse is located at 1000 East Duncan St. in Manchester.

If...

GENEALOGY
From "Old Letters, Papers, Documents, and Photographs Relating to the Limpert Family,"

by Frank Alvin Limpert, July 27, 1937,
Royal Oak, Michigan, U.S.A.

From Dr. Ludwig Limpert, aged 79, and residing at Nuremberg, I obtained the earliest dates and information concerning the family, which is of Frankish origin.

FRANKISH LIMPERT FAMILY

1. Balthasar Limpert von Homburg on the Main River. Born 1640 'de Summerhausen', and married Anna Barbara. **Children:** Two sons, Johannes, born 1660, and Wilhelm,, born 1672, died Feb. 28, 1728. Johannes married Anna Maria, born 1652 and died May 27, 1709, and had 3 children. Johannes was killed by falling from a building in Wertheim on Aug. 8, 1728, where he was working as a master stone mason.

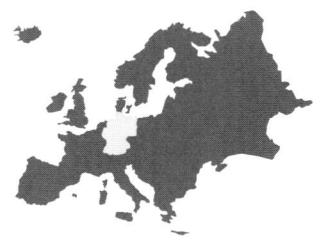

Children of Johannes Limpert:

1. Petrus, born at Homburg in 1681; married Jan. 21, 1710 to Anna Marg Kapfelmann, born July 29, 1682, died Feb. 22, 1737 at Holzkirchen. He died at Holzkirchen, Feb. 19, 1751; 5 children.

2. Anna Maria, married Val Krimm, Sept. 24, 1715 at Homburg.

3. Maria Barbara, married Joh. Adam Sturmer, Jan. 21, 1727 at Homburg.

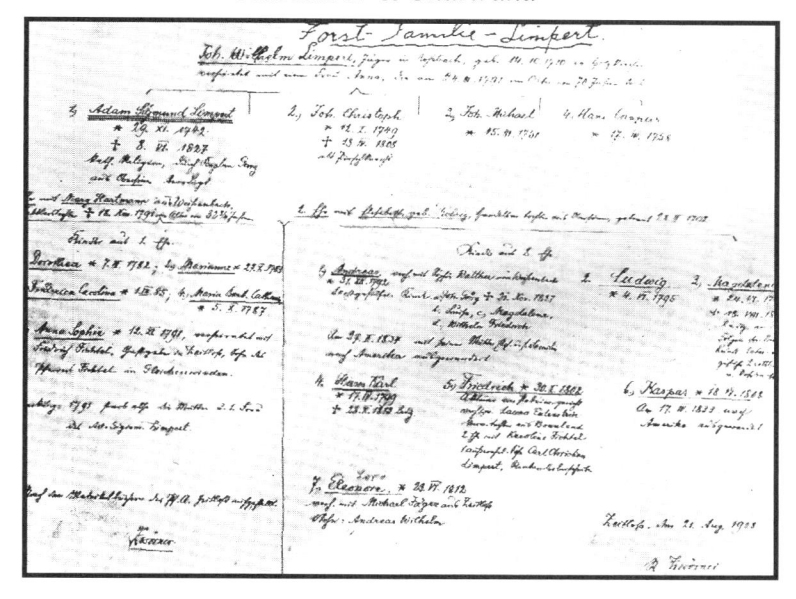

FOREST LIMPERT FAMILY

1. Joh. Wilh., born at Holzkirchen, Oct. 14, 1710. Received his diploma from the Prince-bishops, at Wurzburg, after 2 years of attendance there; received a coat-of-arms and became a member of the Forst-Hoheit or royalty, 207 years ago. Oct. 5, 1730, at the age of 20—the beginning of 'Forst-Family-Limpert'. He became district forester of the barony of Thungen with residence at the mountain village of Rossbach. William married May 1, 1740, and 4 sons were born. Died at Rossbach on Sept. 14, 1776, age 67.

2. Maria Magd. Born Aug. 27, 1713; married Thomas Romisch von Holzhirchen, born Dec. 21, 1728 – died Oct. 20, 1759.

3. Joh. Nik., born July 23, 1716 – died Sept. 27. 1717.

4. Joh. Kil., born Aug. 10, 1718 – died Nov. 7, 1718

5. Mar. Eva, born March 10, 1721; married Joh. Georg Assner, of Grensserheim.

Children of Joh. Wilh. Limpert:

1. Adam Stegmund, born Nov. 29, 1742 at Rossbach

If...

– died there June 8, 1827, at age 85.
  2. Joh. Christoph., born Jan. 12, 1749 – died April 13, 1808. Forester's helper.
  3. Joh. Mich., born March 15, 1751 – died ...
  4. Hans Kaspar, Born April 17, 1758 – died ...

Adam Siegmund, the eldest son, as stated above was born in November, 1742, 195 years ago, in the small village of Rossbach nestling among the hills and mountains of lower Franconia or Unter-Frenken. He spent his boyhood in that locality, and when 18 years of age he went away to Wurzburg to study under the Bishop-princes there, where his father had attended before him. On March 10, 1763, he received his testimonial or diploma at Wurzburg, after three years of attendance there, at age 21. Thereupon he became the helper of his father, John William, hunter and royal forester of the Barony of Thungen district. When about 38 years old, Siegmund married Marg Hortman, saddler's daughter from the neighboring village of Weissenbach age 22. Eleven years of married life slipped by when the young wife died at 33 leaving five daughters, the youngest only six days old.

  On Feb. 28, 1792, in his 49th year, he married again. This marriage with Elizabetha Roehrig, age 20, merchant's daughter of Obsersinn was Protestant; the husband leaving the Catholic religion through the influence of Chaplain Ganz of Obersinnn. Their married life continued until his death 35 years later; seven children (five boys and two girls) being born to them. When Adam Siegmund Limpert died in 1827, age 85, he left twelve children (five daughters by the first wife and seven children by the second) and his widow, Elizabetha, age 55.

Children of Adam Siegmund Limpert:
First marriage, Catholic
  1. Dorothea, born March 7, 1782.
  2. Marianne, born October 27, 1783.
  3. Frederica Carolina, born September 1, 1785.
  4. Marie Barb. Catherine, born October 5, 1787.
  5. Anna Sophie, born November 12, 1791; married Fredrich

Fichtel of Zietlofs.

Second Marriage, Protestant

1. Andreas, born at Rossbach, December 31, 1792 – died at Scio near Ann Arbor, Michigan, June 25, 1860.

2. Ludwig, born April 5, 1795 – died at Bavaria, August 19, 1869.

Elisabetha Limpert and son Andreas

3. Magdalene, born June 24, 1797, at Rossbach – died Aug. 18, 1818, at 21 years of age.

4. Hans Karl, born April 17, 1799 at Rossbach – died of rabies, age 20, October 28, 1819.

5. Friedrich, born January 30, 1802, at Rossbach.

6. Kaspar, born at Rosbach, June 18, 1808 – died at Groveport, Ohio, September 19, 1879.

7. Eleonore (Lora), born at Rossbach on June 23, 1812; married Michael ager of Zeitlofs – died at Scio, near Ann Arbor, Mich. On Oct. 23, 1893, at age 81.

The mother of the above mentioned children, Elizabetha Limpert, died at Ann Arbor, Mich., March 28, 1863. Age 91. (Born at Obersinn on December 23, 1772.

Caspar Limpert, the youngest son, was 19 when his father died in 1827. He had been at school, as his father and grandfather before him, and continued until mid 1831, at Wurzburg, leaving that city for forester's work at Weissenbach, where the earliest letters that I have were written. The reasons for Caspar's coming to America are revealed in these early letters, viz: eagerness to migrate to the new world, American, of which there was great talk in Europe then, and disappointment in his first love affair. He left the old world port of Bremen on April 17, 1833, on a sailing vessel; and arrived about six weeks later at Baltimore. This young man of 25 was the first of the Limpert family in America and was destined to remain here the rest of his life, some 45 years. He traveled over much of the country

If...

when it was an untamed wilderness, was in California in 'gold rush' days of '49 and, in fact, saw the conquering of a virgin continent. In 1848 he married Cynthia Rarey (born 1825 – died 1892) of Groveport, Ohio.

Children of Caspar Limpert:

   1. William Rarey, born April 4, 1845 – died Dec. 17, 1895. Unmarried.

   2. Elizabeth "Zinka" Frances, born Feb. 6, 1849 – died Mar. 28, 1937, at Groveport, Ohio, age 88. she married Thomas Klein Durboraw, of Virginia; a Confederate soldier, in middle life; no children.

   Caspar's meeting at the wharf in Baltimore, 1834, with his mother Elizabetha, his older brother Andreas, his younger sister Lora, and other relatives must indeed have been 'precious'. His description of that event in the unfinished letter to his friend William, dated April 29, 1835, Ann Arbour, MI, and how in his eagerness to embrace them he climbed up the ropes from the wharf to the ship, is something which impressed me more, probably than anything else in his papers which interests me now, nearly 60 years after his death.

Lizzinka "Zinka" Durboraw, daughter of Caspar

   Caspar methodically kept a copy of the letters he wrote in his youth, and some of the earlier ones were found by me in an old trunk. In one of them to his best friend, William, he wrote, "The reading over of our letters of friendship and their answers will in the gray-age (later years) afford us great pleasure." I believe that he did read at least some of these old letters over again in his old age, as there are marks of punctuation, etc. added in pencil on their ink-written pages.

AMERICAN LIMPERT FAMILY

On Feb. 27, 1834, Andreas Limpert, age 42, with his mother, age 62 (Elizabetha), his wife Sophie and four children, Luise, age 13, Magdalane – 7, William Fr. –9, Karl (Charles) – 5, his sister Lora, age 22, her husband Michael Yager, and son Andreas, left their fatherland for America to meet the son and brother, Caspar, who had been there about a year.

Children of Andreas Limpert:

   1. Joh. Georg, died November 21, 1827.

   2. Luise, born at Rossbach on May 7, 1821 – died at Ann Arbor, Mich. She married Philip Muellig; 3 children: William – never married; Sophie – married Wm. Herz, one son, Oswald; Caroline – married J. Gwinner, children, Robert, Emilie – married S. Dieterle, children Robert and Hilda – Mrs. Waterhose. Luise's husband died; in 1857 she married Peter Brehmn; three children: Emma – married T. Hutzel, Elizabeth – married C. Bauman, and son August.

   3. Wilh. Fredr., born at Rossbach, Aug. 15, 1825 – died at Nakusp, B.C., Canada on July 9, 1913; age 88. He grew up on his father's place on Scio Church road a few miles s.w. of Ann Arbor. On Jan. 1, 1854 he married Catherine Sager, born Jan. 3, 1831 – died at Owosso, Oct. 21, 1861, age 30.

Children of Wilh. Fredr. Limpert:

   1. Louis Theodore, born at Ann Arbor, Mich., Oct. 12, 1854 – died at Tampa, Florida on Feb. 3, 1935; age 80.

   2. Henry, born at Ann Arbor, in 1856 —died in Colorado; married; no children.

   3. William, born at Ann Arbor on April 7, 1860 – died of typhoid on April 2, 1883, age 23.

   4. Charles, born at Owosso, Mich. On Oct. 7, 1861; married Sarah Walz; now lies in Lakeland, Florida; children: Ina – married Martin Almendinger, Robert, the one son, lives at Washington, D.C.; Florence – married, no children.

Wm. Fr. Limpert married Again, M. Hass of Ann Arbor, and two children were born at Owosso.

   1. Frederick, born 1863 – died at Couer D'Alene, Idaho, July 28, 1935; married Grace Hatfield, no children.

If...

2. Emma, born Nov. 19, 1865; married Mr. Rowe, deceased; one son, Earl, died. Died at Birmingham, Mich., October 19, 1937.

"The Prairie Rider" from William Frank Limpert's collection

The second wife of Wm. Fr. Limpert died: in 1870 he went to Fife Lake, Kalkaska County, and took up a farm. About 20 years later he went West with his son Fred and traveled over much of Oregon, Idaho, Montana, Washington territory, and was for many years located at Arrow Lake and Deer Park, British Columbia.

On May 10, 1887, at Ann Arbor, Mich., Louis T. Limpert married Lulu Hangsterfer (born March 14, 1860 at Ann Arbor – died June 19, 1932 at Tampa, Florida). His early years, after his mother's death in 1861, were spent with his aunt Luise Brehm, at Ann Arbor, and with his aunt Magdalene Kalmbach, at the old farm in Scio. In 1872, at the age of 17, he traveled by train to Traverse City, via Cadillac, and from there by stage-coach to Fife Lake to his father's. The month was March, and he often told how there was deep snow up north. It was night when the coach reached Fife Lake and the driver pushed young Louie's trunk off into the snow and said, "Here you are, this is Fife Lake." He saw a dim light in the distance and found, upon arriving there, it was his father's log cabin. Eventually he went to Cheboygan, Mich., which was a booming lumber town in those days, and learned the watch-making and jewelry business. Later, he had a jewelry store at Ann Arbor and then at Tampa, Florida. The last 15 years of his life were spent at his home not far from the city of Tampa, raising chickens, oranges and grape-fruit.

Children of Louis and Lulu H. Limpert:

1. Frank Alvin, born Oct. 6, 1889 at Ann Arbor

2. Lillian Elizabeth, born at Ann Arbor - married Carl Bauman; three sons: Clement, John, and Winfield.

3. Katherine Hangsterfer, Ann Arbor – unmarried.

Frank A. Limpert spent his boyhood and youth at Ann Arbor, graduating from the city high school in 1909 and from the University Dental Department on June 12, 1912. He worked in the dental office of Dr. F.W. Woods in Hillsdale for nine months after graduation; and then opened his own office in Detroit, Mich., March 6, 1913. For three years he was part time public school dental inspector, under Dr. Charles Oakman, of the Detroit Board of Health. He married Doctor Oakman's secretary, Iva May Bryant, July 5, 1915 at St. Paul's Episcopal Cathedral in Detroit. On June 17, 1926, he married Mary Edna Stambaugh (born Feb. 1, 1902) at Groveport, Ohio.

Children of Frank Alvin Limpert:

First marriage

1. Alvin Bryant, born July 12, 1916 at 156 Lothrop, Detroit.

Second marriage

1. Donald Edwin, b. Groveport, Ohio, May 7, 1927.

2. Frank Albert, b. Royal Oak twp. Sept. L3, 1929.

3. Frederick Louis, b. Royal Oak twp. Feb. 26, 1932.

4. Marjorie Lucille, b. Royal Oak twp. Jan. 28, 1934.

5. William Erich, b. July 28, 1936, Providence Hospital, Detroit.

If...

EPILOGUE
Don's exposé

When I first approached Don about doing a biography about his life, he immediately joked to friends that we were engaged in putting together an exposé about Manchester and all its political doings. However, when it came right down to it, there were many, many stories that Don, despite his brash teasing, did not want in this book.

Like many individualists, Don has two sides. Our perception of him depends on which side we were most exposed to. Those of us who love and respect the man embrace the knowledgeable and insightful side of this one of a kind, self professed black sheep. We take the harsh no-holds-barred side with a respectful grain of salt. That's why I need to point out that it was Don's idea to tell his story without rehashing past conflicts or passing judgment on those who found themselves on the opposite side of the political fence. He was the one who nixed all the ingredients for a real exposé.

Don was and still is somewhat of a mystery both to friends and, I suspect, even some of his family members. The many people in Manchester who have known him over the past 45 years would, I'm sure, readily agree that they weren't always sure of his motives. He is first and foremost a businessman from the old school; no quarter asked, none given. Business is business and the idea is to make a profit from it. With a few rare exceptions, Don always does.

What made him stand out from the crowd was how he combined his business sense with a rare flair for creativity. His style of renovating old buildings is widely copied and imitated, but never matched. He is an original.

Whatever opinion one has of his years in Manchester, no one worked harder than Don did. Whether he was stripping paint off the storefronts with a putty knife and propane torch, chipping plaster off brick walls, or laying brick and block, Don's work ethic was also old school. He got things done.

He also delighted in his "out of step with society" persona. Many people, like my father, would grin and shake their heads as they watched Don at the city dump filling his truck with items others were throwing away. Many of those items would end up in his antique store with a hefty price tag. Despite his financial success, Don never flaunted it. No fancy home, no big estate. Wherever he lived, however briefly, was shaped for the better by that ceaseless, creative mind.

The purpose of this book is to preserve the legacy of a "one of a kind" rare individual.

25 YEARS LATER:

1981
The 1981 photo of Don on the mill porch was taken by Vern Otto, a Chelsea-based photographer. He happened to be passing through while Don was working and just snapped the picture. Next thing Don knew, it was blown up and in Vern's front display window.

2006
*Same rascal, same pose, same hat.
[Photo by Karl Racenis]*

If...

Afterwords
Manchester Central Business District

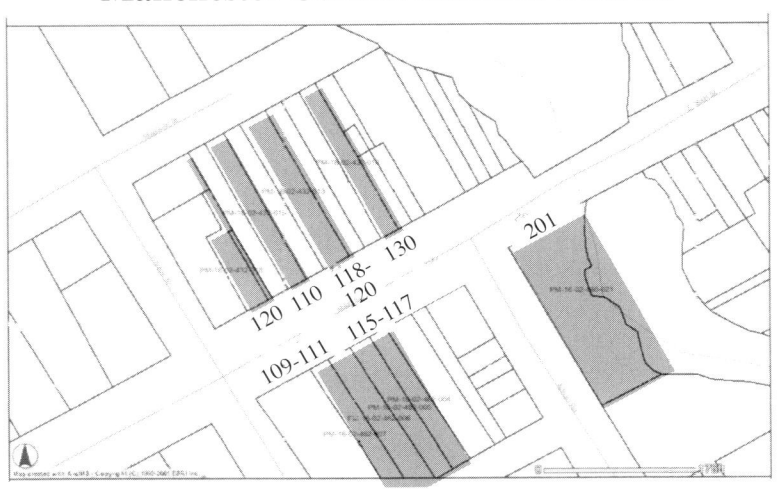

Don Limpert's projects in Manchester between 1966 and 1985 area listed here from the nomination information provided to the Washtenaw County Historic District Commission.

Before Purchase • After Rehabilitation • 2009 Tenant

109 E. Main
    Vacant   Offices   DVD Revolution
                                                                        Manchester Floors

111. E. Main
    Vacant   Ann Arbor Savings   United Bank & Trust

115. E. Main
    Vacant   Black Sheep Tavern   Coffee Mill

117 E. Main
    Sportsman Bar   Black Sheep Tavern   Unforgettable Photos

201 E. Main
    E.G. Mann
    & Sons Mill   Manchester Mill   Manchester Mill

104 E. Main
    Vacant   Antique Shop   Frank's Restaurant

110 E. Main
    Marx & Marx
    Store   Antique Shop   Flower Garden

118 E. Main
    Manchester   Manchester   Manchester
    Bakery   Bakery   Bakery

120 E. Main
    Vacant   Roller Jewelry   Manchester
                                                           Bakery

130 E. Main
    Vacant   Krauss Pharmacy   Manchester
                                                              Pharmacy

Other Affected Projects and Communities:

Before Purchase • After Rehabilitation • 2009 Tenant

324 E. Main, Manchester, MI
    Storage   Blacksmith Shop   Manchester Area
                              Museum   Historical Society

18875 W. Austin, Manchester, MI
    Vacant   Atlas Mill   Manchester
                                                              Feed & Supply

104 W. Michigan, Clinton, MI
    Vacant   Clinton Inn   Clinton Inn

In the foreground are the four buildings Don owned on Main Street's south side-- from left, 117, 115, 111 and 109 E. Main.

If...

National Trust for Historic Preservation's Position on Sustainability

Historic preservation can – and should – be an important component of any effort to promote sustainable development. The conservation and improvement of our existing built resources, including re-use of historic and older buildings, greening the existing building stock, and reinvestment in older and historic communities, is crucial to combating climate change.

Sustainable Stewardship of our Buildings and Communities
Guiding Principles:

• Reuse existing buildings: Use what you have. The continued use of our existing buildings reduces the amount of demolition and construction waste deposited in landfills, lessens unnecessary demand for energy and other natural resources and conserves embodied energy (the amount of energy originally expended to create extant structures).

• Reinvest in our older and historic communities: Older and historic communities tend to be centrally located, dense, walkable, and are often mass-transit accessible – qualities celebrated and promoted by Smart Growth advocates. Reinvestment in existing communities also preserves the energy embedded in infrastructure, such as roads, water and sewer lines.

• Retrofit our existing building stock: Many historic and older buildings are remarkably energy efficient because of their site sensitivity, quality of construction, and use of passive heating and cooling, while other buildings require improvements to reduce their environmental footprint. Historic buildings can go green without compromising historic character.

The National Trust's commitment

Focus on Local, State and Federal Policy: The National Trust for Historic Preservation will work with several cities to develop model policies that encourage preservation as sustainable development. This work will include refining building, energy and zoning codes, as well as developing model language for comprehensive plans and climate change action plans. We will also work to expand the availability of historic tax credits at the state and federal level, encourage other financial incentives for building reuse and community revitalization and support energy policy that improves energy efficiency in older buildings.

Empower Preservation Practitioners: The National Trust will provide our network of practitioners with the tools they need to incorporate green building practices into their preservation work. This will include development and dissemination of best practices and other guidance for greening older and historic buildings.

The peaceful setting along the mill pond of the River Raisin has made this real estate a coveted address in Manchester for more than 30 years. The original Mill Pond apartments had five units. Don lived in one closest to the River Raisin.

The Union Savings Bank (now Comerica Bank) was one site of many of Don's struggles with local politicians. James C. Hendley, a local attorney, was one of Manchester's "kingpins" in the 1950s through 1970s, and was a proponent of the urban renewal effort that ended up tearing down the Dresselhouse and Davidter Hardware building before Don could rescue it.

To this day, Limpert is fond of saying that putting a modern 1970s facade on the main level of the Union Savings Bank building was like "giving a face lift to a 90-year-old woman."

Barn-lumber strips created faux cross beams in many downtown buildings, and some of those touches remain intact in today's businesses

The Sportsman's Tavern, later the Black Sheep, was housed in the building in the foreground at 117 E. Main Street. A colorful mural is now painted over the spot on the building where the Dresselhouse and Davidter Hardware was torn down to make way for a drive-in bank lane.

If...

Above: *This residence at 415 E. Main Street had fallen on hard times in the 1970s, until Don purchased the house and restored it to its former glory.*

Left: *A hole in Manchester's Main Street remains 40 years later where the Dresselhouse and Davidter store once stood*

On his own

Don Limpert accomplished gigantic preservation efforts without the benefit of an Historic District Ordinance. He did not have the dictates of public policy to direct him. If he had submitted to such dictates, one wonders if things might have turned out differently or if he and the U.S. Secretary of the Interior might have had the same standards in common. The following "standards" are often referred to, in the historic preservation business as "The Ten Commandments."

The United States Secretary of the Interior's Standards for Rehabilitation

The Standards (36 CFR Part 67) apply to historic buildings of all periods, styles, types, materials, and sizes. They apply to both the exterior and the interior of historic buildings. The Standards also encompass related landscape features and the building's site and environment as well as attached, adjacent, or related new construction.

Rehabilitation projects must meet the following Standards, as interpreted by the National Park Service, to qualify as certified rehabilitations eligible for the 20% rehabilitation tax credit.

The Standards are applied to projects in a reasonable manner, taking into consideration economic and technical feasibility.

1. A property shall be used for its historic purpose or be placed in a new use that requires minimal change to the defining characteristics of the building and its site and environment.

2. The historic character of a property shall be retained and preserved. The removal of historic materials or alteration of features and spaces that characterize a property shall be avoided.

3. Each property shall be recognized as a physical record of its time, place, and use. Changes that create a false sense of historical development, such as adding conjectural features or architectural elements from other buildings, shall not be undertaken.

4. Most properties change over time; those changes that have acquired historic significance in their own right shall be retained and preserved.

5. Distinctive features, finishes, and construction techniques or examples of craftsmanship that characterize a historic property shall be preserved.

6. Deteriorated historic features shall be repaired rather than replaced. Where the severity of deterioration requires replacement of a distinctive feature, the new feature shall match the old in design, color, texture, and other visual qualities and, where possible, materials. Replacement of missing features shall be substantiated by documentary, physical, or pictorial evidence.

7. Chemical or physical treatments, such as sandblasting, that cause damage to historic materials shall not be used. The surface cleaning of structures, if appropriate, shall be undertaken using the gentlest means possible.

8. Significant archeological resources affected by a project shall be protected and preserved. If such resources must be disturbed, mitigation measures shall be undertaken.

9. New additions, exterior alterations, or related new construction shall not destroy historic materials that characterize the property. The new work shall be differentiated from the old and shall be compatible with the massing, size, scale, and architectural features to protect the historic integrity of the property and its environment.

10. New additions and adjacent or related new construction shall be undertaken in such a manner that if removed in the future, the essential form and integrity of the historic property and its environment would be unimpaired.

If...

You are not alone

Anyone impressed with Don Limpert's great commitment to historic preservation and his accomplishments in Manchester may well wonder how they can find a clone of him to save their deteriorating downtown commercial district. Although it will be difficult to find so much talent in a single individual, there are plenty of organizations that specialize in just those creative dynamics:

- **Washtenaw County Historic District Commission**
    (12 different Historic Districts)
    Melissa Milton-Pung, Principal Preservation Planner
        734-222-6878 (eWashtenaw/historic preservation)
- **Ann Arbor Historic Preservation**
    Historic Preservation Coordinator
    Jill Thacher, 734.794.6265 x 42608
        Admin. Service Specialist to the HDC
    Brenda Acquaviva, 734.794.6265 x 42666
        Planning & Development Services
        100 N. Fifth Avenue, Ann Arbor, MI, 48104
        hdc@a2gov.org
- **Saline Historic District Commission**
    Jeff Fordice, Staff Liaison, Recording Secretary
        (jfordice@city-saline.org) 429.4907 ext. 2225
- **Ypsilanti Historic District Commission**
    Planning and Development Department
        734.483.9646 (hdc@cityofypsilanti.com)
- **Michigan Historic Preservation Network**
    Nancy Finegood, Executive Director
        107 E. Grand River Avenue, Lansing, Michigan 48906
        517.371.8080   Fax: 517.371.9090
        info@mhpn.org   www.mhpn.org
- **Michigan State Historic Preservation Office**
    Michigan Historical Center, P.O. Box 30740,
        702 W. Kalamazoo St., Lansing, MI 48909-8240.
        517.373.1630 (preservation@michigan.gov)
- **National Park Service**
    Historic Preservation Planning Program
        (NPS_Hps-info@nps.gov)
- **National Trust for Historic Preservation**
    5 Massachusetts Ave. NW, Washington, DC 20036-2117
        202.588.6000 or 800.944.6847 fax: 202.588.6038

A quick glance at today's bakery counter could easily be mistaken for a scene from 40 years before.

Here, at 109 and 111 E. Main, an enclosed garden area surrounds the entrance to upper-level apartments.

Manchester's downtown has been irrevocably shaped by Don Limpert's vision over a period of nearly 45 years.

If...

Harry Macomber Writing—from essays, short stories, poems, screen plays and many letters to the editor—has been Harry's main love his entire life. His book, "How The Bee Got Inside My Bib Overalls..." was published for the Pittsfield Township Historical Society in 2005. Currently residing on his horse ranch in Tennessee, he continues to indulge that love of writing. He can be reached at: harrymac@dtc-com.net

Marsha Johnson Chartrand, a Manchester-area resident for 40 years, first met Don Limpert when looking for an apartment in downtown Manchester in 1976. She subsequently followed both his progress and history in the community as a freelance writer, staff reporter and eventually Editor of the *Manchester Enterprise* from 1991-2006. She has served as a Village Planning Commissioner with Don and currently is a member of the Manchester Village Council. She continues to write about Manchester topics for local publications and is delighted to be collaborating with Harry Macomber and Tom Dodd on "IF..."

Tom Dodd, our editor and cheerleader, has published Ypsilanti's *Depot Town Rag* since 1976. He has retired from fifty years of teaching art and journalism at Eastern Michigan University, Ann Arbor Community High, and Washtenaw Community College. He serves as chair of the Pittsfield Township Historical Commission and collaborated with Harry Macomber's on his "Bee Book" for the Pittsfield Township Historical Society.